DRUG COURT

ABOUT THE AUTHORS

Mitchell B. Mackinem

Doctor Mackinem is currently an Assistant Professor of Sociology at Claflin University. He comes to academics after twenty years of working in the addictions treatment field. Doctor Mackinem has worked as a frontline addictions counselor in a variety of settings including residential treatment program for probationers and for the past ten years been involved with drug court. Doctor Mackinem has made many presentations at national and regional meetings in sociology and criminal justice with several publications forthcoming. He currently uses his experience in addictions and criminal justice to inform his academic work on problems-solving courts, court alternatives, and deviance.

Paul Higgins

Paul Higgins is a professor of sociology at the University of South Carolina, Columbia. He has published more than a dozen books and monographs about deviance, disability and sociology, including works concerning deaf communities, rehabilitation professionals, educating together deaf and hearing students, the puzzles of social life, thinking about deviance, and the school-year experiences of an elementary school student. He and Mitch Mackinem have written and published about adult drug courts.

DRUG COURT

Constructing the Moral Identity of Drug Offenders

By

MITCHELL B. MACKINEM, PH.D.

Department of History and Sociology
Claflin College
Orangeburg, South Carolina

and

PAUL HIGGINS, PH.D.

Department of Sociology
University of South Carolina
Columbia, South Carolina

CHARLES C THOMAS • PUBLISHER, LTD.
Springfield • Illinois • U.S.A.

Published and Distributed Throughout the World by

CHARLES C THOMAS • PUBLISHER, LTD.
2600 South First Street
Springfield, Illinois 62704

ISBN 978-0-398-07800-3 (hard)
ISBN 978-0-398-07801-0 (paper)

Library of Congress Catalog Card Number: 2007046283

With THOMAS BOOKS *careful attention is given to all details of manufacturing and design. It is the Publisher's desire to present books that are satisfactory as to their physical qualities and artistic possibilities and appropriate for their particular use.* THOMAS BOOKS *will be true to those laws of quality that assure a good name and good will.*

Printed in the United States of America
LAH-R-3

Library of Congress Cataloging-in-Publication Data

Mackinem, Mitchell B.
Drug court : constructing the moral identity of drug offenders / by Mitchell B. Mackinem and Paul Higgins.
p. cm.
Includes bibliographical references and index.
ISBN 978-0-398-07800-3 (hard) -- ISBN 978-0-398-07801-0 (pbk.)
1. Drug courts--United States. 2. Drug abuse--Treatment--Law and legislation--United States. I. Higgins, Paul C. II. Title.

KF3890.M33 2008
344.7304'46--dc22

2007046283

PREFACE

"All rise," calls the burly deputy sheriff to those present for drug court on a Tuesday night in the capital city of a southeastern state. A loud knock on the wooden wall behind the judge's bench accompanies the command, signaling the start of court.

So begins *Drug Court: Constructing the Moral Identity of Drug Offenders*, a richly detailed field research investigation of how drug court professionals work to help drug offenders become drug free and law abiding. Drug courts are the latest approach in America and in other countries for handling problem drug users. More than 1,500 drug courts exist throughout the United States and its territories. They developed out of and continue the shifting emphasis on punishment and treatment of problem drug users in America and elsewhere. Critics caution that with the aim to treat drug offenders, drug courts may not adequately safeguard the rights of the offenders when they are punished.

Based on more than five years of field research in three drug courts in a southeastern state in the United States, in two of which the senior author was the drug court administrator, *Drug Court* explores how the team of drug court professionals transform drug offenders into drug court clients. Judges, administrators, drug counselors, lawyers, and others compose the drug court team. However, "you never know who will make it" successfully through the program, say drug court professionals of the drug offenders.

Drug courts are intended to treat addicts who commit crimes due to their addiction, not primarily criminals who happen to use drugs. Therefore, drug court professionals face the challenge of deciding whether drug offenders are primarily criminals who have little, if any, desire to kick their habit or are drug abusers who will work to go straight. Are the drug offenders appropriate clients for drug courts?

Are the drug court clients participating adequately within the drug court program? Have the drug court clients performed successfully in the program to graduate?

Through their evaluation, interpretation, monitoring, sanctioning, and more, drug court professionals judge the moral worth of drug offenders as they treat and manage the offenders through drug court. *Drug Court: Constructing the Moral Identity of Drug Offenders* is the "behind-the-public-scenes" story of how drug court professionals perform this complex work. It is a story of hope and it's loss and of hope once again.

M.B.M.
P.H.

ACKNOWLEDGMENTS

We gratefully acknowledge the generous contributions of all the drug court professionals involved in this book. Their trust in us and this project is humbling and has made this book possible. Mitch also wants to acknowledge the continued support of his family and his wife, Beth. Paul appreciates the support from his wife Leigh and his daughters for all of his writing.

CONTENTS

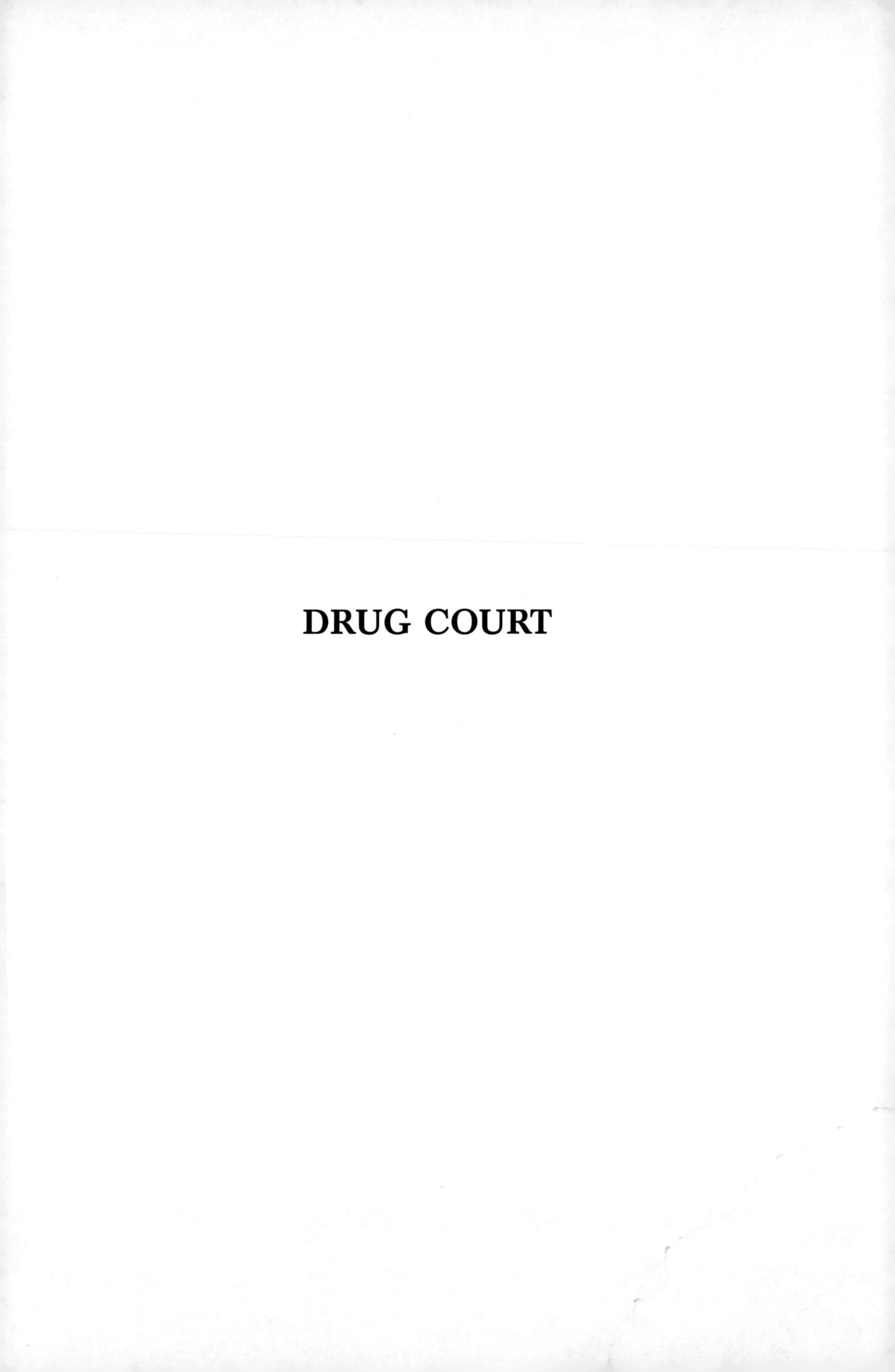

DRUG COURT

INTRODUCTION

"All rise," calls the burly deputy sheriff to those present for drug court on a Tuesday night in the capital city of a southeastern state. A loud knock on the wooden wall behind the judge's bench accompanies the command, signaling the start of court. The fifteen or so men and women who are clients in drug court, sitting and chatting in clusters in the audience, stand as do the half-dozen family and friends who accompany some of the clients. The drug court administrator and treatment providers, sitting at one of the two tables before the bench, and the public defender, sitting at the other table, rise to their feet as the presiding judge in his black robe appears behind the bench and quickly sits. Flanked by the state flag and seal and the American flag, Judge Brook peers down at the crowd in the three-hundred-seat, wood paneled courtroom. The judge looks at the drug court administrator, who begins the call of clients.

"Your honor, I need to inform the court that Mr. Burt Hill and Ms. Betty David have disappeared," states Mr. Mackinem, previously a long-time drug counselor and now the only continuing professional from when this drug court was established four years earlier. "They have not participated in any services since the last court. Both have a long history of problems in this program. I know Mr. Hill in particular. The public defender has worked extensively with him. Given that they have had problems and have disappeared, the prosecuting attorney's office is requesting that Mr. Hill and Ms. David be removed from the program."

After the public defender states her agreement to this action, the drug court administrator continues in a conciliatory tone, "Your honor, if the public defender's office finds some kind of mitigating circumstances, we would review this matter in the future."

"Okay," replies Judge Brook, a respected circuit judge with more than ten years of experience, who volunteered to preside over this and a nearby drug court.

"Your honor, I would like to call Mr. Bernie Brown," Mr. Mackinem tells the court. As Mr. Brown walks to the front of the courtroom to stand at the microphone before the judge, the drug court administrator continues, "Mr. Brown tested positive for cocaine. He admits it. He knows he did it. I was teasing him earlier that drug court ruined the high for him. It wasn't any fun; he didn't enjoy it. He felt guilty about it. We are recommending that Mr. Brown do eight hours of community service."

"I will accept the recommendation and require you to do eight hours of community service. Let us look for a better report next time. I am glad you did not enjoy it," Judge Brook replies with a faint smirk. The crowd is quiet as Mr. Brown returns to his seat without making a comment.

"Your honor, I would like to call Robbie Black," Mr. Mackinem states. "Mr. Black is not in the middle of a horrendous relapse. He is in the middle of a long relapse. He keeps saying that he is trying to get it together. He did sign up for Green Village, which will take him. However, we are very concerned about his traveling, hanging out with women who are using drugs while trying to reconcile with his girlfriend. There isn't any stability in his life. The recommendation is that he stay in jail until he goes to Green Village. This could be three, possibly four, weeks away. We do recognize that he has financial obligations–his apartment, lights and things. He does work two jobs. We have done what we can do with him. He can't seem to stop. He has a good attitude. He does not skip meetings. He is not hostile. He is in the middle of a relapse. He thinks addictively. He has a secret fantasy that if he goes somewhere else, the addiction will go away. Nothing bad, your honor, nothing horrible. He can't seem to stop, and he can't seem to clean up."

"Alright, any idea about what is going on?" the judge addresses Mr. Black, who now stands at the microphone before the bench, staring at the floor, with deputies flanking him.

"I do not want to be in jail, your honor," replies Mr. Black. "I have a lot of bills to catch up on. I guess I have been hanging with the wrong people. It has caught up with me. Since my girlfriend moved out, I need the extra money to pay the bills. She made a lot more money than I did, judge. I don't plan on doing it again."

"If you go to Green Village, will you lose your job?" Judge Brook asks.

"No, sir."

"I will not put you in jail at this time. The next time we have court, if you have another positive test, I am going to do it. Not jail time to punish you, but jail time to protect you from yourself," the judge explains to Mr. Black.

"Your honor, in the last month, Robbie has received no punishment for his positive drug tests, for his missed tests," interjects Mr. Mackinem, knowing that this client is slipping by without the usual sanctions. "We had hoped that Green Village would come along. I would recommend that some type of sanction be given. He has received nothing."

"Alright, no question," responds the judge to the administrator's explanation. "What I will give him is 48 hours in jail. When do you want to do it, Mr. Black?"

"Anytime, your honor," replies the drug court client.

"You need to go to jail this weekend. Next time you will get more jail time," chastises the judge.

"Friday night at 6, your honor?" questions Mr. Mackinem as he fills out the court order.

"Friday at 6 P.M. till Sunday at 6 P.M.," replies Judge Brook.

As the drug court clients and their family members and friends stir in their seats, the drug court administrator continues to call clients forward to stand before the judge.

"Your honor, I would like to call Mr. Mike Gray. Mr. Gray is no longer at the halfway house. There was some interpersonal conflict," explains the administrator, having been told by the client that some of the residents had accused him of being gay, which reportedly created too much conflict for the client to take. "It could not be resolved, and Mr. Gray returned home. He went to the emergency room last night. We decided to do a drug test because Mr. Gray always goes to the emergency room right after he uses or when he is using in order to cover it up. We did do a drug test. Mr. Gray voided into the cup and then put cold water in the cup in an attempt to fake his test. The counselor found out that it was cold. Mr. Gray then confessed to having used crack cocaine."

Exasperated, Mr. Mackinem continues, "Your honor, we have sent Mr. Gray to Green Village. He has done jail time. And we have tried the halfway house. Frankly, we are at our end. However, we just found him to be positive right before court and would like to have a little more time to reflect before we make our final recommendation. I recommend jail now. He has no job."

"I do have a job," interrupts Mr. Gray. "I'm a telemarketer."

"Our recommendation is for very significant jail time," the administrator presses on, "from today until the next court session or every weekend until the next court."

"Mike, do you have any idea about what is going on at this point?" Judge Brook addresses the client.

"Yes, sir. Well, quite frankly, I got weak and relapsed. I was going through stress. I started calling someone, and I went ahead and used. I do have a pretty good job. There is no excuse for what I did. I used," Mr. Gray admits softly.

"What I am going to do is, you will spend the next two weekends in jail," declares Judge Brook to the drug court client. "That will allow you to continue to work during the week. If you come back with another report in the same fashion, we are going to talk about something a little more serious. It sounds like to me, and I don't want to misinterpret it, you may be on the verge of being booted out of the program."

"Absolutely!" Mr. Mackinem agrees.

"Well, if that by itself doesn't get you motivated to do it, then you got a bigger problem. With your record, it looks like you have a good chance for jail time. It looks like you either clean yourself up or go to prison. I think I know which one I would pick," warns the judge.

"You honor, I see Ms. Epps in the courtroom. I had not seen her earlier. She was supposed to graduate tonight. Instead, I am recommending that she do four hours of community service because she tested positive for marijuana," the drug court administrator tells the court, disappointed that this college senior had not yet cleared her record so she could become a teacher.

"Sorry," responds Judge Brook, "you got to the point you were ready to graduate. I will accept the recommendation and give you four hours of community service. Don't let it slow you down."

"I won't," replies Ms. Epps, head down, disheveled.

"If I were perfect, I would give you a hard time, but I am not. Just work past it," the judge gently admonishes the client. "Keep working toward where you are going. I know you can get there. Let's look for a better report next time."

"Thank you," Ms. Epps replies softly, her eyes puffy.

"Your honor, I would like to call Holly Burke," Mackinem informs the court. "Miss Burke is charged with a drug crime. We all are recommending that she be admitted to the drug court program." The administrator was deliberately vague about her drug habit, because he feared that since the client was in the middle of a custody fight, any of her drug court records could end up in divorce court.

"Good. It's good to have you in the program," Judge Brook tells the client, who stands before him. "I think you will find, I know you will find, that everyone in this room wants you to succeed. No one wants you to fail." Pointing toward the administrator and the treatment providers, the judge continues, "They have done this with a lot of people. They know what they are doing. They will have recommendations from time to time. There is always a reason for it. They will have you do some things from time to time. You won't enjoy it, but they know what they are doing. Hopefully, we won't have to use sanctions. But if it ever comes to that, I want you to know that there is a reason for it. We are not trying to hassle you or give you a hard time." The audience applauds as the judge concludes his remarks to the new drug court client.

Turning to the successful clients, Mackinem proudly informs the judge, "Your honor, Mr. Belk tested clean on all his tests." Over the next several minutes, the administrator informs the judge of clients who have tested clean on their drug tests, attended counseling, are being moved to more advanced phases of the program, or in other ways are doing well in the program. The judge congratulates the clients, and the audience applauds them.

Coming to the highlight of the court session, the administrator tells the court, "Your honor, we have one person graduating tonight. I would like to call Mr. Knight. Mr. Knight is not the kind of a man who just jumps right in. He is a very cautious and thoughtful person. I can say that when Mr. Knight first came into the program, he sat on the side. He wasn't sure he really wanted to get in. He didn't do anything bad, nothing like that. He just wasn't sure he wanted to jump in. Is that fair to say?"

"Yeah, that's right," Mr. Knight replies.

"I don't know what happened," continues Mackinem. "He probably could answer that. Then one day, he just jumped right in. Once he made the decision that he wanted to be in the program and be sober, he's just done great. Everything is not over. There are still some struggles. He is an independent businessman, and that is hard. But he is not going to use. I know that, and he knows that."

Solemnly and with pleasure, the administrator concludes, "So, it is the recommendation of the prosecuting attorney's office that since Mr. Knight has met all the requirements of the program that he be allowed to graduate and all charges against him be dismissed."

"Congratulations. It gives me pleasure to give you this certificate. Good luck," Judge Brook warmly tells Mr. Knight after leaving his bench to shake the client's hand. The audience's applause fills the courtroom.

"I'll keep it short and sweet," states Mr. Knight, who is expected to make a few remarks upon graduating from the drug court program. "The thing that got me going was you (pointing to the drug court administrator) were going to kick me out of the program. I decided I better do what I was supposed to do." The drug court clients gently laugh.

"I want to thank the staff, the drug court administrator, the court, and all of you," Mr. Knight ends to the applause of the court.

"Your honor, that's it for tonight" Mackinem concludes, "except to recognize three of our graduates who are sitting in the courtroom." The administrator introduces the three graduates of drug court, who stand and are thanked by the judge for coming. With the exit of Judge Brook, drug court ends this night in one southeastern city.

Judge Brook's drug court is one of the more than 1,500 drug courts operating in all states and territories in United States, with another 391 in planning (Cooper, 2005; Justice, 2006).[1] England, Australia, and other countries have their own versions. These popular court-supervised drug treatment programs are one of the most recent attempts by the criminal justice system to manage illegal drug use. They have handled more than 300,000 drug offenders since the first one was established in 1989 (Cooper, 2003). Drug courts are also controversial. Critics contend that legal safeguards for protecting the accused may be jeopardized in the attempt to help drug-using offenders (Nolan, 1998, 2001, 2002).

Outside of the public drug court session, a composite instance of which opened this book, is the less visible work of drug court administrators, treatment professionals, prosecutors, public and private defense attorneys, judges, and other professionals. Through investigation, interpretation, deliberation, negotiation, monitoring, sanctioning, treatment, and judgment, these drug court professionals transform drug-using offenders into drug court clients. Approximately half of the clients nationwide will succeed, graduating from drug court (Belenko, 2001). We explore how committed professionals work with drug-using offenders and with each other to help drug-using offenders quit their use. It is a story of hope and hopelessness. It is a story of how drug court professionals attribute moral identities of worth and worthlessness to drug-using offenders.

CONSTRUCTING MORAL IDENTITIES

When people interact, they attribute identities to each other. They

---

1. All names of drug court professionals, except for Mitch Mackinem's, and clients in this and subsequent instances are pseudonyms.

decide whether the others are smart, kind, manipulative, competent, deceitful, caring, shy, domineering, and whatever other qualities they may give to the others (Higgins, 1994; Sandstorm, Martin, & Fine, 2003). People may at first tentatively attribute identities to others. Later, they may be more definite in their attributions. Their attributions affect future interactions. The competent, kind individual is approached for help and advice; the manipulative, deceitful individual is avoided and others are warned about that untrustworthy person.

People may agree or disagree about who the other is, about what kind of individual the other is. People will often assume that their understanding of the person is right, those who differ are wrong. They assume that those who have attributed different identities to the person are not sufficiently perceptive or have not adequately interacted with the person to know who that person really is.

People typically assume that everyone has "inside of them" their identities, their "who-they-are." These "inner" identities may change over time as people develop. When people decide who others are, they assume that they are more or less accurately seeing who the others are. Of course, others may try to pretend, deceive or hide their true selves. The competent observer knows this and will be alert to others' manipulated presentations of self (Goffman, 1959). We might call this an essentialist view of identities (Roy, 2001).

A different approach to identities does not assume that individuals have "inside" them their "true" identities. Instead, people always construct identities for individuals out of their interactions with the individuals and out of how they give meaning to experiences. No identity construction is right or wrong because there is no true identity against which to evaluate the constructions. However, the identities given by observers may differ greatly with profoundly different consequences. If a jury decides that the guilty murderer is a heinous individual, then the jury may sentence the convicted murderer to death. If the jury decides that the guilty murderer is a repentant offender who was a victim of a deplorable childhood, then life in prison may be the sentence. From this non-obvious view of identities, an important question is: How do people construct identities for others and with what consequences (Higgins, 1994)? This constructionist view of identities guides us in our discussion of how drug court professionals judge drug-using offenders as the professionals do the work of drug court.

In order to do their job, drug court professionals attribute identities to drug-using offenders, to drug court applicants and clients. The professionals decide who these offenders are. How truthful are the offenders? How sincere are they in their desire to stop using drugs and to quit committing crimes? How capable are they of succeeding in the program? Are they trying to recover or are they "playing games"? Are the offenders largely problem drug users who commit crimes as part of their drug use and who now have a sincere desire to stop using drugs and to cease committing crimes? Drug court professionals view such offenders as morally worthy of their efforts and limited resources. Or, are the drug-using offenders someone other than that? Are the offenders primarily criminals who also use drugs with no sincere interest in stopping either their criminal behavior or their drug use? If so, then drug court professionals see these offenders as morally unworthy of their efforts and resources. Still other drug-using offenders may be understood by drug court professionals as problem drug users who do not presently have the ability to stop their drug use. These users have not yet "hit bottom." The professionals may exclude these offenders from the program or reluctantly dismiss them from the program after they have been admitted.

Drug court professionals who shared their experiences with us and who allowed us to observe their work assume that deciding who drug-using offenders are is difficult. Mistakes may be made in deciding who is appropriate for the program. Identities initially attributed may need to be revised as the professionals work with the offenders. Drug court professionals believe that they cannot be certain how a drug court client will perform in drug court. While they will not accept every drug-using offender, they will give a chance to offenders who appear to have a reasonable hope of succeeding, who appear to be worthy of the drug court program. When drug court professionals lose hope, when they decide that the offenders are either not sincere or not capable at present of stopping their drug use, the professionals eliminate the offenders from the program. In the chapters that follow, we explore how drug court professionals in three drug courts in a southeastern metropolitan area–in Urban, Suburban and Farming counties–judge drug offenders, how they create moral identities for the offenders, as they work to help the offenders quit their drug use.

Drug court professionals do not take a constructionist view of their work. They view drug offenders as having a true identity, which may be difficult to determine and about which they may honestly disagree.

With dedication and sincerity, they try to evaluate, treat and judge drug offenders as professionally as they can. We do not intend our use of a constructionist view to demean the essentialist view that drug court professionals and most people use. Our constructionist view may enable us to develop understandings that will benefit all who are interested in understanding drug courts.

While we explore the judgment of drug offenders, the creation of moral identities for applicants and clients is not unique to drug courts. This process occurs throughout criminal justice and human service organizations (Bell & Campbell, 2003; Douglas, 1970; Emerson & Paley, 1992; Frohmann, 1991; Goode, 1984; Gubrium & Holstein, 2001; Mather, 1979; Prottas, 1979; Snow & Anderson, 1993; Vogler, 1993; Weppner, 1983). In deciding how to use their limited resources, human service and criminal justice professionals decide what kind of applicant, client, accused, victim or other service seeker stands before them: Are the applicants for vocational rehabilitation services sincere in the desire to improve their employability (Higgins, 1985)? Is the homeless woman a troublemaker at the shelter (Liebow, 1993)? Are the youth charged with delinquency "good" kids who were just "fooling around" (Sanders, 1976)? Our story about the construction of moral identities in drug court can inform and be informed by the work exploring identity construction in other human service and criminal justice organizations.

WHAT FOLLOWS

In Chapter 1, we discuss how the United States has historically managed problem drug use through a shifting emphasis on punishment and treatment, with both approaches being used concurrently. Each approach provides a different moral identity for problem drug users. Punishment provides an identity that is less morally worthy than does treatment. Since the crack epidemic of the late 1980s, drug courts have developed within that ongoing tension. We explore how the media, drug court leaders and local programs have portrayed drug court. We explore the effectiveness of drug court, and, finally, we present the concerns drug court critics express regarding its legal underpinnings.

We provide in Chapter 2 an overview of the drug court process through which drug court professionals manage drug-using offenders.

Through a sequence of organizational actions and decisions, the drug court staff accepts or rejects drug-using offenders into the program; treats, monitors and sanctions them through the program; and then decides whether the drug court clients have successfully completed the program. We also explore the organizational positions and concerns of the drug court professionals–the prosecuting and defense lawyers, program director, treatment providers, and judge. While their organizational interests and professional training differ, the drug court professionals typically collaborate to manage drug offenders.

Chapters 3, 4 and 5 are the core of the book. In Chapter 3, we discuss in detail the admission process for drug court. How do drug court professionals evaluate drug offenders, deciding whom to admit into drug court and whom to reject? The number of drug offenders eligible to enter the drug court programs that we studied far exceeded the capacity of the programs. With limited resources and with a concern for how admission decisions might reflect on the prosecutor's office, drug court professionals make uncertain decisions about which drug offenders are worthy of the program and which offenders are too risky or do not have sufficient potential to succeed. Drug court professionals did not accept the casual user who would benefit from existing and less intensive programs even though doing so may have led to a greater success rate for the program. Neither did the professionals accept those drug offenders who were understood to have insufficient motivation or capability to participate effectively in the program or posed an unacceptable risk to the treatment staff or to the viability of the program. Drug court professionals judge the potential of the drug offenders.

Chapter 4 explores how drug court professionals monitor, evaluate and sanction drug court clients as the clients move through the treatment program. Clients may participate for a few days to a year or more. They attend group counseling, are drug tested, and regularly appear in court before the judge. The judge may send clients to jail for a weekend or order them to perform community service when they fail to meet the requirements of the program. As they succeed, they may be promoted to a less intensive phase of the treatment program and are commended in court. Drug court professionals judge the clients' participation. Are the clients "working a program of recovery" even if at times they experience setbacks, or are they just "playing games"? Are they addicts who are trying to become abstinent or are they criminals trying to deceive the professionals? As drug court professionals monitor the progress of the clients, they move beyond only evaluating the clients' behaviors to attributing more encompassing moral identities to the clients.

In Chapter 5, we examine how drug court professionals decide whether drug court clients have successfully completed the program or whether they will be removed from the program. The professionals judge the clients' performance. Drug court professionals do not remove clients who have missed a counseling session or tested positive for drug use. Failures and setbacks are expected. However, when drug court professionals begin to believe that clients will not succeed at this time or when the professionals decide that clients are "worthless," then the professionals proceed to remove the clients from the program. Drug court professionals challenge clients who are on the verge of being removed from the program with trials to show that they are working toward recovery. But as hope is lost, the professionals build a case for removing the clients from the program. For clients who succeed, graduation from drug court is a ritual of celebration for the clients and the drug court staff.

We summarize in the Epilogue the key understandings we have developed about the social construction of moral identity in drug court. As drug court professionals manage drug-using offenders through the program, they create organizationally specific identities for the offenders. The professionals create identities for the offenders that speak to the purpose of the program, not to the rich and varied experiences of the offenders as persons. The drug court professionals reduce people to more or less worthy clients. The professionals create these moral identities within the larger debate in society about problem drug users. We also emphasize that drug courts and their staff produce the successes and failures and all other outcomes that occur. The conduct and the characteristics of the drug court applicants and clients do not in and of themselves produce the drug courts' results. Within drug court policies and procedures, the staff makes the decisions that record the behaviors of the drug-using offenders as what they officially come to be. We encourage those who explore other problem-solving courts to examine how staff does the work of those courts rather than be satisfied with program design studies or statistical evaluations. Finally, we respond to critics' concerns that, with an emphasis on therapeutic jurisprudence, the good intentions of drug court professionals may lead to unjustified legal jeopardy for drug users.

Drug court professionals gather and evaluate information as part of their work with drug offenders. In the Appendix, we discuss how we "gathered and evaluated information," how we researched over several years three drug courts in one southeastern metropolitan area. Being a drug court administrator provided Mitch Mackinem an invaluable opportunity to develop an insider's view of drug court. However, being an insider also proved to be challenging for exploring drug court. Mitch's colleague, Paul Higgins, is an experienced field researcher who is not a drug court insider. As a team, we benefited from being both an insider and outsider. Just as we view drug court professionals as constructing the moral identities of drug offenders, we see field researchers as constructing the story of their scene. In the Appendix, we explore how we did so.

What follows is a story of drug court professionals, not drug-using offenders or drug court clients. Naturally, offenders and drug court clients populate drug courts and this book. However, the drug users exist in this book through the eyes–and the identity constructions–of the drug court professionals. We now turn our attention to America's historical management of problem drug users and to the recent rise of drug courts.

Chapter 1

MANAGING PROBLEM DRUG USERS: THE RISE OF DRUG COURT

In Miami in the 1980s, cocaine rained from the sky. Pursued by airborne agents of the Drug Enforcement Agency, drug traffickers from South America in small prop planes dumped their load of cocaine over Dade County in order to avoid arrest. Miami became flooded with this cheap, highly addictive drug. Drug arrests soared, overwhelming the Miami jails and courts. The criminal justice system responded by quickly arraigning drug offenders, setting low bail bonds, and rapidly releasing those arrested. It became common for officers to see on the streets offenders they had arrested an hour earlier for possession of crack cocaine (Murray, 1999). This revolving justice regarding drug offenders grew intolerable. Something different needed to be done.

The Chief Justice of the Florida State Supreme Court asked the Honorable Herbert Klein to explore alternative judicial responses to the increasingly overwhelming problem of drug crime. Klein concluded that traditional legal processing would be ineffective for holding back the floodwaters of drug offenses and offenders. Drug treatment was promising, but the high rates at which offenders dropped out limited its success. Klein decided that combining the court system with drug treatment might succeed. If drug-using offenders could be coerced to become drug treatment clients, then offenders and the city's intolerable drugs-and-crime problem may change (Terry, 1999a).

Miami's and the nation's first drug court began in the summer of 1989. Judge Stanley Goldstein, the first drug court judge in the nation, and other local officials did not intend to reform the entire judicial system. Instead, they were attempting to respond to vast amounts of cocaine and the attendant problems inundating their city (J. Goldkamp, 1999).[1] Other drug courts soon arose in Oakland, California; Broward County, Florida; Portland, Oregon; Maricopa County, Arizona; and Las Vegas, Nevada, among other places (Terry, 1999b).

Drug courts have developed rapidly and widely in the United States since the first court in 1989 in Miami. The number of drug courts grew to 42 by 1994, to 161 by March 1997, and to nearly 1,100 in 2004, covering all 50 states(Cooper, 2001; Huddleston, Wilson-Freeman, Marlowe, & Roussell, 2005).[2] Similarly, federal funding for drug courts has increased markedly from an initial 6 million in 1993 to a proposed 70 million in 2007 (National Drug Court Institute, 2004). This funding to local jurisdictions for the development and operation of drug courts has been a major spur for their dramatic growth.[3]

Since the Civil War, America has struggled with how to handle users of mood-altering chemicals. Drug courts are part of this country's ongoing attempts to handle problem drug users. While some politicians and journalists have characterized America's policy toward problematic drug use as a "war on drugs," America has never had a single policy. Instead, America has always been of at least two minds regarding drug abuse and those who abuse drugs. According to Steven Belenko, a reoccurring theme has been the tension between the "medical" approach to controlling drugs and the "punitive" enforcement approach (Belenko, 2000).

America's policy toward problem drug users has always been a shifting mix of help for the sick drug abuser and punishment for the drug-offending criminal. Historically, during times of heavy criminalization, new treatment programs began; conversely; during times when treatment was emphasized, punishment initiatives proliferated.

The tension in America's policy toward problem drug use rests on

1. The Miami Drug Court handled approximately 1,300 drug offenders its first year. Only 4% of clients were arrested for new drug crimes while participating in the program (Haigney, 1990.)
2. Drug courts have become an international movement. The International Drug Treatment Court Association has members throughout the world with its board representing 9 different counties including Australia, Britain, Brazil, and Canada (Bentley, 2005).
3. Beyond this direct funding of drug courts by federal grants, designated block grant monies, administered by the state, are for drug court use. These local block grants include the Local Law Enforcement Block Grants and the Bryne Memorial Block grant (Tauber, Weinstein, Allen, & Lieupo, 2000).

how America has identified its problem drug users, both individually and collectively. Are problem drug users sick drug abusers who are morally worthy of help or committed criminals who also happen to be drug offenders who should be punished? Drug courts are a recent development within this ongoing tension in America's policy toward problem drug users. Like the policy of which it is a part, drug courts, too, reflect that tension. Who are the drug offenders who have come to drug court?

To understand drug court and how the professionals in drug court work with drug-using offenders, we first present in this chapter a brief overview of the history of America's response to problem drug use, explaining the shifting emphasis on punishment and treatment. Next, we explore different portrayals of drug court as offered by federal agencies, officers of associations of drug court professionals, brochures explaining drug court, and the media presenting drug court to the public. Collectively, these portrayals reflect the tension between treatment and punishment, between the drug user as worthy addict or unworthy criminal. Third, are drug courts effective in combating drug use and criminal behavior among drug-using offenders, as their supporters tout? We summarize the research investigating drug court's effectiveness. Finally, we present the moral warrant for drug court and a concern about that warrant. Drug courts draw their moral warrant from therapeutic jurisprudence, a legal philosophy that holds that the justice system can and should operate to make the offender and the community "healthier," not merely to punish the transgressor (Hora, Schma, & Rosenthal, 1999). Critics of therapeutic jurisprudence, however, are concerned that in the desire to assist the worthy drug addict, drug courts may not safeguard the rights of the criminal (Nolan, 2002). We conclude by emphasizing that drug court is not a revolutionary development in American policy toward problem drug use, nor is it immune from the tension in American policy between treatment and punishment of drug offenders. To the contrary, drug courts embrace both the treatment and punishment of drug offenders, using the latter to facilitate the former but only for those who are the worthy drug users.

PUNISHMENT AND TREATMENT: AMERICA'S RESPONSE TO PROBLEM DRUG USE

America's policy toward drugs has varied throughout its history. It has tolerated, promoted, prohibited, punished, and treated drug use. Punishment and treatment have been intertwined in America's response to problem drug use, with a shifting emphasis on one or the other.

Before the 1900s, citizens, respectable and disreputable, had easy access to a wide variety of mood-altering substances through patent medicines. Opium, cocaine, and marijuana were all readily available, with no legal restriction (Morgan, 1981). Opium was prescribed for many illnesses and often described as "God's Own Medicine" (Belenko, 2000).[4] With the widespread use of opium and patent medication, the number of people addicted began to grow to an estimated 250,000 during the Civil War and immediately thereafter (Musto, 1999).

The opium user was feeble-minded, a hapless victim of the drug or a sinister threat depending on the user's racial and cultural identity. The war veteran who treated his wounds with morphine or the housewife who used a "tonic" to treat menstrual discomfort were pitied and helped (Belenko, 2000). Lower class people were ordered to institutions for the feeble-minded. However, Chinese immigrants who smoked opium and often ran "opium dens" were threats to America's way of life (White, 1979).

As the century came to a close, the issue of drug use and drug users changed from a matter for families, doctors and local communities to a national crisis. Newspaper articles on the evil of drug use and the Chinese threat appeared and sustained the growing public fear of drug use. In response to these fears, Congress acted. The Food and Drug Act of 1906 required patent medicines to list ingredients so that individuals would not be duped into addiction. During this same period, Congress passed the Opium Exclusion Act of 1909 and the Foster Anti-Narcotic Bill of 1910. Both bills portrayed drug use as a product

4. For more detail on the history of drug policy, drug control and drug treatment, we recommend: Steven Belenko's *Drugs and Drug Policy*, David Musto's *The American Disease: Origins of Narcotic Control* and William White's *Slaying the Dragon: The History of Addiction Treatment and Recovery in America.* Drawing from a wide range of primary sources, Belenko constructs a dynamic picture of America's changing policies toward drug use. Musto's book is a comprehensive review of American drug control activities, while White's book is a complete history of drug treatment in America.

of a foreign menace, particularly the Chinese (Musto & Korsmeyer, 2002).[5]

In 1914, Congress passed the single most important law in the history of drugs, the Harrison Narcotic Act (Musto, 1999). This law and subsequent court rulings had a major impact on American drug policy for the next fifty years. Partly out of a fear of non-white drug users and an equal fear of an underworld, this federal law eventually made it illegal for doctors or pharmacists to prescribe narcotic drugs for nonmedical purposes (Inciardi, McBride, & Rivers, 1996). The formerly respectable drug users who had been under doctor's care now became criminals.

The importance of the Harrison Narcotic Act quickly became evident as the normal sources of opium, morphine and cocaine dried up. The sick and the duped had to struggle to meet their addiction needs. According to a New York Times article of the period, "the poor addicts were having a pretty tough time of it." They often unknowingly bought fake drugs out of their desperation and pain (Belenko, 2000).

The Harrison Narcotic Act was not unopposed. The American Pharmaceutical Association and the American Medical Association actively opposed the act. A strong voice for the medical treatment of addiction and opposing criminalization was that of Doctor Charles Terry. Believing that addiction is a medical, not legal, issue, Terry advocated the use of medical clinics. He established the first opiate maintenance clinic in 1919 in Jacksonville, Florida. It was founded out of the community's concern over the plight of poorer addicts. The medical clinics provided a safe, reliable source of narcotics for the sick habituate to function normally. New York State followed, establishing numerous clinics, which were opened at the encouragement of both the federal government and the state Department of Health. At their height in popularity, more than 100 clinics operated in the country (Musto, 1999). After extensive federal inspection, investigation and harassment, the last clinic closed in 1923.[6]

---

5. According to William White, drug scares occur within a common propaganda methodology. Various federal and state officials create drug scares. White sees such strategies as rooted in the nineteenth century prohibition movement and appealing to many deep-seated cultural fears. Similarly, Reinarman and Levine illustrate how the TV media promoted the "crack scare" and how politicians subsequently used this fear to promote a conservative political agenda under the Reagan administration (Reinarman & Levine, 1997).

6. *Doremus vs. U.S.* supported the arrest of physicians for the prescription of opiates for nonmedical purposes. This Supreme Court decision provided the full legal authority for closing clinics.

Clinics and drug maintenance were not the only efforts to treat drug addicts and abusers; hospitals and anti-drug clubs also provided aid. Willmar State Hospital in Minnesota opened for the treatment of inebriates in 1912, declaring that addicts were patients in need of medical care. In anti-drug clubs, common throughout the United States, members tried to help each other and the public in general to confront the problem of drug use. White Cross Clubs formed in the western states of America in 1921. Their sole purpose was to help members quit narcotics and to promote anti-narcotics efforts in their communities. While the Harrison Narcotic Act identified users as criminals, other federal, state and local agencies and individuals defined addicts as patients in need of medical attention. Future federal approaches toward problem drug users followed a similar pattern, meting out punishment and offering aid, though in widely varying mixes (Musto, 1999).

One consequence of the Harrison Narcotic Act was the incarceration of many new offenders because they were drug addicts. Wardens of the federal prisons at Atlanta and Leavenworth reported in letters and hearings for the proposed Porter Act that two-thirds of all prisoners were drug addicts (Belenko, 2000). Criminal justice professionals saw the lack of treatment for these new inmates as a serious problem. With great support from criminal justice professionals, the Department of Justice, and medical professionals, the Porter Act of 1929, while making heroin illegal in any form, established two federal narcotic farms for the treatment of addicts. The Porter Act also established a new category of addicts; the criminal client, an addicted criminal offender, coerced to receive needed treatment. As with the modern drug court, the Porter Act attempted to force drug offenders to change their drug-using behavior.

In 1935, the same year the Lexington Narcotic Farm opened, Alcoholics Anonymous (AA) was started in Ohio and was formed when two struggling alcoholics, Bill Wilson and Doctor Robert Smith, met for mutual support (White, 1998). Alcoholics Anonymous stands as a major innovation in the treatment of alcoholism. Its impact and importance are hard to overestimate. Problem drinkers could now get help in church basements in almost any town or city across the country. The problem drinker could become a recovering addict, a new identity with less stigma.

America's response to problem drug use in the 1940s and 1950s continued to be a mix of punishment and treatment. During the peak of the Cold War and the "McCarthy Hearings," several studies pointed to the increasing importation of drugs from Mexico and China, and most importantly from Sicily where the Mafia operated laboratories to convert opium into heroin. Teenagers were understood to be the latest victims of these foreign sources of drugs. In response, the Federal government increased the penalty for drug importers. In 1951, Congress passed the Boggs Act, which established minimum mandatory punishment for drug smuggling. Shortly after the Boggs Act, the American Bar Association and various medical associations all questioned the wisdom of increasing punishment without help for the addicts on the street (Belenko, 2000). This pressure led to increasing Federal support for treatment efforts.

In the late 1940s and the first part of the 1950s, methadone and Antabuse were introduced as new medications in the treatment of addictions. Methadone limited the cravings for opiates like heroin and morphine without offering the euphoric effect of natural opiates. Discovered in 1947, Antabuse has no effect on humans unless they ingest alcohol (White, 1998). In the presence of alcohol, Antabuse produces strong negative side effects for the subject. As a result, doctors widely prescribed Antabuse to alcoholics in the hope that the negative side effects would deter them from using alcohol.

The development of Narcotics Anonymous (NA) and the "Minnesota Model" for addiction treatment in the late 1950s became important for the treatment of drug addicts. Narcotics Anonymous was developed by an active AA member who felt the need for drug users to gather in mutual support (White, 1998).The development of the Minnesota Model took place over several years in three closely-related facilities in Minnesota: Pioneer House, Hazelton and Willmar. All three facilities used AA "recovering" staff to provide services. Over time, the AA approach to residential treatment became refined and called the Minnesota Model. The Minnesota Model remains a dominant model of addiction treatment.[7]

As the 1950s were coming to a close, one final development that had profound impact on the future of addictions treatment was a new version of residential treatment, the Therapeutic Community. "TCs," as they were termed, are now the dominant model of prison-based

7. The Minnesota Model began as a model for residential treatment; however, this model was rapidly modified for outpatient services.

treatment. They grew out of the work of a recovering addict, Charles Dederich, who mixed the principles of AA with some of the newer group therapy methods of confrontation. A well-researched approach, Therapeutic Communities remains a viable part of drug treatment for criminal addicts, but not for middle-class addicts (Tims, De Leon, Jainchill, & National Institute on Drug Abuse, 1994).

Another drug scare out of which came an increased, but not universal, emphasis on treatment and a prolonged period of "drug toleration" marked the 1960s and 1970s (Musto, 1999). In 1973, President Richard Nixon, borrowing language from Lyndon Johnson, declared a war on drugs. The war declaration grew out of renewed fears of drug use. Heroin, which had not been common since the late 1920s, resurged in popularity. Marijuana became widely available. Finally, a new drug, LSD, moved from experimental use to common illicit use.

Middle-class youth were viewed as the tragic victims of this new drug epidemic. In 1969, Diane Linkletter, the daughter of Art Linkletter, a notable TV personality with his hit show, "Kids Say the Darndest Things," jumped from a balcony window. At the time it was widely reported she was under the influence of LSD, although this later was disputed (Mikkelson & Mikkelson, 2003). If the daughter of a beloved figure like Linkletter could die because of drugs, was any teen or young adult safe? Such stories, whether or not true, changed the identity of the drug user. While the scary image of black urban heroin users was still popular, drug users in large part were seen as middle-class children who needed help, not unworthy social outcasts (Musto & Korsmeyer, 2002).[8]

Unlike in response to the drug scare at the turn of the century, Congress, at the urging of many, responded with increasing emphasis on treatment. Congress passed many Acts in response to the drug problem, including the Narcotic Addict Rehabilitation Act of 1966, the Alcoholic and Narcotic Addict Rehabilitation Act of 1968, and the Drug Abuse Office and Treatment Act of 1972. All these Acts created and organized professional drug treatment for users of mood-altering chemicals. Drug treatment became more available. The Minnesota

8. In 1973, then Governor Nelson Rockefeller pushed the passage of a series of laws that harshly punished drug use and sale. For example, all people caught selling more than 2 ounces of marijuana must serve a mandatory minimum of 15 years in prison. Referred to as the "Rockefellar laws," these laws, later repealed or modified, represented a movment away from the then national trend toward tolerance and treatment.

Model became the treatment standard. States opened publicly funded residential programs and clinics.

This period of tolerance and treatment led to the legislative discussion of decriminalization of marijuana. The drug advisor to President Carter, Doctor Peter Bourne, in concert with National Organization for the Reform of Marijuana Laws (NORML), moved to decriminalize marijuana. The effort ended when Bourne was dismissed due to writing questionable prescriptions for methaqualone tablets for an aide and due to rumors of using cocaine at a NORML party (White, 1998).

During the 1970s, a precursor to drug courts, the federally supported Treatment Alternatives to Street Crime (TASC) was developed to coerce identified alcohol and drug using defendants and criminals into treatment. TASC programs were created through a federal grant program designed to "demonstrate the full use of the criminal justice system's coercive powers to reduce drug use and related criminal activity" (Birmingham, 2001). TASC initially targeted first-time offenders, later handling offenders with more extensive criminal records (Inciardi et al., 1996). By creating close alliances between traditional criminal justice entities like prosecutors or probation officers and the drug treatment centers, TASC set a foundation for future drug courts. TASC continues to operate some drug courts.

The 1980s was a time of extreme luxury and poverty in treatment. As drug addiction became less stigmatized, insurance companies began to offer drug treatment coverage in their policies. Luxury treatment programs quickly grew with the availability of insurance money, previously never a major source of treatment funding. Private programs with chefs and located in beautiful estates became common. For example, a former mayor of Washington D.C. was caught on videotape using powder cocaine. While certainly disgraced, he went to a luxury treatment program, not prison. With increasing restrictions for the insurance industry, such luxury treatment all but disappeared by the early 1990s (White, 1998).

At the same time as this luxury treatment, AIDS made its deadly appearance. Intravenous drug use, the preferred route for heroin use, is quite effective in transmitting the HIV virus. The focus on AIDS prevention led to a renewed interest in drug addiction treatment for IV users. Many IV users lived desperate, impoverished lives. They spread the HIV virus in "shooting galleries," alleyways, and abandoned buildings, common grounds for some IV use. Public and private nonprofit agencies tried many public health efforts to reduce the use of heroin, including needle exchange and methadone maintenance, far from the luxury treatment offered to the insured. This period of toleration came to a crashing end in 1985 (White, 1998).

In the early 1980s, powdered cocaine became the new popular drug. Often portrayed as a "glamour" drug and popular in the disco party scene, cocaine was initially thought not to be physiologically addictive, or at worst, to be only "psychologically" addictive. The comedian Richard Pryor's famous self-emulation while free-basing cocaine helped change the glamour image. In 1985, the newest version of cocaine, crack, became widely available. Highly addictive, crack quickly became the dominant drug (Inciardi, 1992). HIV fears, the crack epidemic–widely seen as a scourge of the black community–and the resurgence of highly potent marijuana led to several major laws that cracked down on illicit drug trafficking, selling and use and provided some treatment to users (Alexandrova, 2004).

The Anti-Drug Abuse Act of 1986 put $4 billion toward the drug problem, with 70 percent going toward interdiction efforts by law enforcement and the remainder going toward expanded treatment efforts. Punishment and treatment, once again, were America's mixed response to problem drug behavior. It is at this moment in history, a moment where crack users overwhelmed communities, jails and treatment centers, that drug court appears.

PORTRAYING DRUG COURT

When asked by those not involved in drug court to explain what it is, Mitch often replied that drug court is a court-supervised drug treatment program. While lacking detail, Mitch's description captures the collective portrayal of drug court found in brochures, letters to victims of drug offenders, federal publications, pronouncements by national leaders of drug courts, and the popular media. Portrayals of drug court vary from one instance to another and by the audience toward which the portrayals are targeted. Collectively, the portrayals embody the tension between punishment of the offender and treatment of the addict. Within the collective portrayal of drug court are several elements. Drug courts are tough (better than traditional approaches) and they provide hope, with a new, even revolutionary, team approach that integrates legal and treatment means for dealing with offenders who are drug users.

Drug court program brochures, widely-circulated within local law enforcement communities, tell interested parties what to expect in drug court. Mitch observed several brochures on bulletin boards in a local jail. The following excerpt from a brochure that describes the Urban County drug court emphasizes the significant requirements that participants in the program must meet.

The program lasts one year or longer. During that year the defendant must:

- Attend three counseling sessions per week
- Attend at least two AA/NA meetings per week
- Drug testing, at least one per week
- Attend court every two weeks
- Avoid all drug use including alcohol

The brochures emphasize that drug court is a series of required activities. Participants are "defendants," who remain under the threat of prison or other punishment.

The letter sent by Urban County's drug court to victims of drug-abusing offenders to inform them of the program and to solicit their approval for their offenders to enter the program states that "defendants who fail to graduate face prosecution." Drug court is not a "soft-on-crime" response.

Drug courts are portrayed as better than the traditional response to drug-using offenders. The same letter sent to victims also states:

> The program is designed to provide an alternative course of legal response to drug and drug-related crimes. The alternative legal response provided by drug court is both quicker than the traditional legal response and thus there is a short period of time between arrest, jail, and legal action. Further, by diverting less serious offenders to an alternative legal response, the drug court enables more specific prosecution of serious drug offenders, including major drug dealers.

Thus, drug court makes more sense for the less-serious drug-using offenders and by allowing the criminal court to concentrate on the more serious offenders, drug court helps the criminal justice system to work better for the more serious offenders, too. Speakers at national and state meetings of drug court professionals (attended by Mitch over many years) also emphasized that drug courts were effective in dealing with drug-using offenders compared to the traditional criminal justice approach.

Drug courts also provide hope for a better life for those whose drug dependency has destroyed their lives and the lives of their loved ones. Media may particularly portray this more personal, human-interest angle of drug court. Newspaper accounts present stories of individual drug-using offenders dramatically, even miraculously, changing their lives through drug court. An article in a local newspaper, "A life changed: The anatomy of a drug court," tells the story of Doris, a young woman who graduated from drug court (Ripton, 2000). Doris had entered drug court with several drug charges. At first she was quite defiant, often telling others that she was never going to quit drugs. By the time of the article, Doris had quit drugs, married, had a young child, and was taking evening classes at a local community college. Similarly, another newspaper article, "Drug court helps addicts regain control of their lives," tells the dramatic accomplishments of another female participant (Hines, 2003). This change was cast in near miraculous tones, portraying drug court as providing possibilities for redemption. Consider the following passage from an article entitled "A five-time washout, this addict broke the cycle" that appeared in the national newspaper *USA Today* (Johnson, 1998).

> Daniels, arrested for possession of crack cocaine, knew what was about to happen and she couldn't have been happier about it. After a review of her file, Judge Stanley Goldstein dispatched her not to jail but to a drug treatment program overseen by the court–even though Daniels had washed out of the program five times before.
>
> Last Friday, nearly ten months after Daniels, 48, appeared in court, she graduated from Goldstein's drug court–free from drugs for the first extended period of time in more than fifteen years.

The article reports that she has a job, has reunited with her two sons, and has her own "modest apartment." All this is possible because she went to drug court, which transformed her life.

Drug court has consistently been represented as a court revolution. In 1997, at the Third Annual National Drug Court Conference in Los Angeles, Judge Jeffery Tauber, then-president of the National Association of Drug Court Professionals, inspired those gathered with his opening speech on the drug court revolution. Drug court would be the catalyst in the court revolution. A 1999 publication by the National Drug Court Institute reported that for "more than a decade, a quiet revolution has occurred within the criminal justice system. Dade County, Florida established the first drug court in the United States. All drug courts are part of an innovative judicial model whereby offenders are held accountable for their actions and afforded the tools they need to break the patterns of drug abuse that so damage their lives, as well as the lives of others" (Freeman-Wilson, 1999). In 2005, the director of the White House Office of National Drug Control Policy announced the revolution is still underway after fifteen years. Drug court is portrayed as a revolution in criminal justice.

The team approach of drug court is presented in an oft-cited document, "Defining Drug Courts: The Key Components," which serves as the fundamental guideline for many developing drug courts (Drug Court Program Office, 1997). Written by a committee formed by the National Association of Drug Court Professionals (NADCP, 1999) and the Office of Justice Programs (OJP), the latter providing federal funding and services to drug courts, the document presents ten key components:

1. Drug courts integrate alcohol and other drug treatment services with the justice system of case processing.
2. Using a nonadversarial approach, prosecution and defense counsels promote public safety while protecting participants' due-process rights.
3. Eligible participants are identified early and promptly placed in the drug court program.
4. Drug courts provide access to a continuum of alcohol, drug, and other related treatment and rehabilitation services.
5. Abstinence is monitored by frequent alcohol and other drug testing.
6. A coordinated strategy governs drug court responses to participants' compliance.
7. Ongoing judicial interaction with each drug court participant is essential.
8. Monitoring and evaluation measure the achievement of program goals and gauge effectiveness.
9. Continuing interdisciplinary education promotes effective drug court planning, implementation, and operations.

10. Forging partnerships among drug courts, public agencies, and community-based organizations generates local support and enhances drug court effectiveness.

Drug courts use a team approach that merges legal and treatment procedures and professionals, that joins prosecuting and defense attorneys into a nonadversarial relation, and that calls on the resources of the community to be effective. The judge is the captain of the team.

As portrayed through a variety of sources, drug courts are new, even revolutionary, tough team approaches for dealing with drug-using offenders that merge legal and treatment orientations and professionals, that work better than the traditional criminal justice approach to drugs and crime, and that provide hope of redemption for drug addicts who commit crimes. Whether revolutionary as some portray them or an outgrowth of previous developments in managing drug-using offenders, are drug courts effective? To that issue we now turn.

THE EFFECTIVENESS OF DRUG COURTS

A large and growing body of research has examined the effectiveness of drug courts. We divide this work into two categories. First, does drug court work? More properly, does drug court work better when compared to other judicial responses such as probation or incarceration? Second, for whom does drug court work?

The body of research assessing the effectiveness of drug court supports one fundamental conclusion: drug court reduces recidivism (Banks & Gottfredson, 2004; Bedrick & Skolnick, 1999; Belenko, 2001; Brewster, 2001; Deschenes & Greenwood, 1994; J. S. Goldkamp, 1999; Goldkamp, White, & Robinson, 2001; Gottfredson & Exum, 2002; Gottfredson, Kearley, Najaka, & Rocha, 2005; Hora et al., 1999; Longshore et al., 2001; Nolan, 2001, 2002; Peters & Murrin, 2000; BJA, 2004; Rempel et al., 2003; Spohn, Piper, Martin, & Frenzel, 2001; SMU, 2002). We discuss a rigorous study in New York State to examine in greater detail the question of drug court's effectiveness (Rempel et al., 2003).

In an oft-cited review, the Government Accountability Office (GAO) criticized the quality of studies evaluating drug court on the basis of several methodological issues including a lack of comparison groups, short-term follow-up, and a lack of multiple-site studies (GAO,

1997). The New York study, a stringent evaluation, does not suffer these shortcomings. The researchers evaluated eleven different courts located throughout the state, including courts in metropolitan, suburban and rural settings. They followed the drug-offending subjects for three years beyond the program completion. At six of the eleven programs studied, the drug court graduates were compared to a matched sample of offenders for each court's population, who received traditional probation services; in the remaining five, graduates were compared to nonmatched samples, such as program failures. The results from each individual court and from all six courts collectively showed that when graduates of drug courts were compared to a matched sample, drug court graduates were less likely to be rearrested. The reduction in recidivism averaged 32 percent. The five courts with nonmatched comparison groups showed similar recidivism reductions. This finding is congruent with findings from seventeen other drug court recidivism evaluations (BJA, 2004). Drug courts reduce rearrest rates for drug-using offenders.

An important issue regarding drug courts' impact on recidivism rates is the retention of clients in the program. The more time that drug abusers spend in treatment, the greater the benefit to the drug abusers (Joe, Simpson, & Broome, 1999; Peters, Hass, & Hunt, 2001; Peters & Murrin, 2000; Peyrot, 1985; Young & Belenko, 2002). Drug courts excel here. Even drug court clients who fail the program may experience positive benefits if their participation exceeded four to six weeks (Peters et al., 2001).

Research that investigates for whom drug court works explores two related domains: client characteristics and program characteristics. First, what type of client characteristics affect program outcome? Second, are some types of treatment philosophies, case management strategies or program component arrays more effective than others? More sophisticated work asks the question, what types of clients do well in what types of programs? In examining for whom drug court works, the studies include drug-court specific research as well as reviews of related research in the addiction and criminal justice fields.

Research results regarding who is most likely to succeed in drug court are diverse and occasionally contradictory. For example, some researchers have concluded that race and gender are related to program graduation with nonwhite and male participants being less likely to graduate compared to white and female participants (Schiff &

Terry, 1997; Senjo & Leip, 2001). However, other researchers have concluded that neither race nor gender is related to program completion (Mackinem, 2003a; Miller & Shutt, 2001; Peters, Haas, & Murrin, 1999; Tauber & Snavely, 1997).

One way to begin to make sense of the diverse, at times contradictory, research concerning what client characteristics are related to program success is to examine the social stability of the drug court client (Peters, Haas et al., 1999). Social stability refers to attachment to conventional others and commitment to conventional means for making a living that may encourage drug court clients to succeed (Hirschi, 1969). Social instability is indicated by unemployment, youthful age, lower income, extensive and diverse criminal history, and frequent relocations (Deschenes & Greenwood, 1994; Goldkamp & Weiland, 1993; Goldkamp et al., 2001; Gottfredson & Exum, 2002; Miller & Shutt, 2001; Spohn et al., 2001). The socially stable are most likely to benefit from drug court, but they do not represent the "typical" drug defendant.

Students of drug court have also discussed and examined differing service delivery systems and their impact (Bouffard & Taxman, 2004; Goldkamp et al., 2001; Longshore et al., 2001; Taxman, 1999). For example, drug court treatment programs with a diversity of staff with differing treatment orientations or staff using no specific treatment orientations will have more unsuccessful outcomes than philosophically consistent drug court treatment programs (Bouffard & Taxman, 2004). Out of specific drug court studies, others have proposed analytic models of understanding drug courts that emphasize interaction between client characteristic, program characteristics and community concerns (Goldkamp et al., 2001). The movement from the original diversionary models to post-conviction models reduces the drug court's impact and may not reduce recidivism, suggesting a further impact that program models may have upon accomplishments (Justice, 2006).

THERAPEUTIC JURISPRUDENCE

As drug courts developed and departed from criminal courts, therapeutic jurisprudence was offered as a warrant for drug court. Therapeutic jurisprudence is "the use of social science to study the extent to which legal rule or practice promotes the psychological and physical well-being of the people it affects" (Slobogin, 1995). Beginning in courts that dealt with mentally ill defendants, therapeutic jurisprudence promotes the use of law to support public policy goals, but not to the exclusion of other considerations, such as evidentiary laws or community safety (Wexler, 1990). Therapeutic jurisprudence counterbalances legal principles such as fairness, equality, and rights with the needs of the client for protection, treatment, and support. Cases are tried in traditional courts; clients are managed in therapeutic courts. In traditional courts a guiding principle is defendant rights; within therapeutic courts the guiding principle is client needs. The therapeutic jurisprudence philosophy moves the court from processing cases to helping clients (Rottman & Casey, 2000). The power of the therapeutic court enhances public good through promoting individual wellness, rather than merely punishing the individual.

As drug courts moved beyond early experiments, several leaders in the movement offered therapeutic jurisprudence as the legal justification for drug court (Hora et al., 1999). Their article was reproduced by the National Association of Drug Court Professionals (NADCP, 1999) and mailed to all its members, an unprecedented event. Consequently, this article became one of the foundations for drug courts.

The movement toward therapeutic jurisprudence and away from traditional court has been contested. Scholars have expressed serious legal concerns with the rise of therapeutic courts in general and drug courts in particular. Berman outlines six categories of concerns: coercion, advocacy, structure, impartiality, paternalism, and separation of power (Berman & Feinblatt, 2001). The first concerns the degree to which defendants voluntarily enter the program. "Are problem-solving courts any more coercive than the practice of plea-bargaining that resolves the large majority of criminal cases in this county?" (Berman & Feinblatt, 2001; 2005). The remainder of the tensions center on the fairness of the judicial process as compared to traditional courts. For example, the departure from the traditional adversarial court system toward a treatment team concept may leave the defendant without an active defense (Boldt, 2002). All key court personnel play diminished or significantly altered roles, which may greatly reduce the role of defense counsels to protect their clients from harsh, unjust court actions (Nolan, 2003; Quinn, 2000; Spinak, 2003).

Traditional courts operate under a philosophy of "just desserts." This philosophy maintains that criminals are to be punished as a result of their criminal act and that the severity of the punishment should be commensurate with seriousness of the offense. In therapeutic jurisprudence, punishment is used as a tool for compliance and thus is not related to severity of the crime. Therapeutic jurisprudence could lead to punishment that exceeds what would be received in traditional court.

The changing role of the judge in drug court may contain specific dangers (Hoffman, 2002b). Judges have great power to punish but are only amateur therapists, opening the opportunity for naïve abuses of power. The judges are not independent but act in concert with others, including private therapy providers who profit by the judge's decisions.

Interestingly, both participants and staff in one study perceived drug court as more equitable and respectful than traditional court (Farole & Cissner, 2005). Participants felt they had a voice in the court; they could and did talk directly to the judge about their concerns and complaints. Treatment, not the court, was the source of most participant complaints. This single study stands in contrast to the procedural concerns of legal professionals and scholars. In the conclusion of this book we take up these criticisms after having explored how drug courts operate.

CONCLUSION

Drug courts are part of America's long history in managing problem drug users. Begun in 1989 in Miami, when that city was flooded with cocaine, drug courts have rapidly spread across America and to other countries. Drug courts embody the tension in America's policy toward problem drug users. That tension reflects the competing identities given to problem drug users: the sick abuser and the drug-using criminal. America has typically helped the sick drug abuser and punished the drug-using criminal.

Portrayed as a revolution in criminal courts and in the handling of drug-using offenders, drug courts have been found to significantly reduce drug use and recidivism compared to traditional courts. However, drug courts are not without their critics, who question whether under the rationale of therapeutic jurisprudence, drug-using offenders' rights and liberties will be adequately protected.

Drug courts use the power of the criminal justice system to coerce drug-using offenders to be treated. Through a complex process, drug court professionals evaluate, treat, monitor, sanction, and remove or graduate drug court applicants and clients. The staff members judge applicants' and clients' potential, progress, and performance in drug courts. As they do so, they identify whether the drug-using offenders are worthy addicts or unworthy criminals. To an overview of the drug court process we now turn.

Chapter 2

THE DRUG COURT PROCESS AND PROFESSIONALS

On a sunny afternoon in early October, Freddy Solomon, a young man in his early twenties with dyed blonde hair and a choker around his neck, arrived at the office of the program coordinator for Urban County's drug court, located in the county judicial center. A few personal photos and posters decorated the walls with file cases, bookshelves and old desks arranged throughout Mitch Mackinem's office. With a brief phone call to Mitch a few days earlier, Bob Tucker, a powerful and respected local attorney, had set the appointment for Freddy Solomon as Freddy sat in Bob's office. Mitch knew that Bob Tucker charged his clients large fees. Freddy Solomon paid $10,000 up front, Mitch later learned. After directing the young man to sit, Mitch asked the crime with which he was charged.

"Distribution of ecstasy," Freddy replied nonchalantly.

Mitch was surprised because charges of dealing and distributing drugs routinely excluded offenders from participation. "Are you sure? Maybe it was Possession with Intent to Distribute (PWID)?" Mitch asked.

"Yeah, dude, I was at the wrong place at the wrong time. I made a bad decision."

Adopting a clinical tone, Mitch said, "Tell me all about it."

"A friend wanted some, and I knew a guy who had some, so I got it and took it over to him. Look, man, I don't do drugs, never have. I just made one mistake, and it has ruined my life. I can't have a (criminal) record. I am applying for these jobs with pharmacy companies. I mean, I am being considered (for a job) as we speak. If I get convicted, it will ruin it all," Freddy explained in a plaintive tone.

"Have you looked into pre-trial (intervention)?"

"Yeah, that is what I need because I can't have a record."

With further questioning, Freddy revealed he had been in pre-trial intervention several years earlier.

Mitch questioned Freddy to learn whether he used drugs and whether he had a drug problem. Freddy refused to reveal any information about drug use. He frequently returned to his main point that he could not have a criminal record. Mitch terminated the interview because Freddy was upset and only wanted to discuss the matter of a criminal record. Mitch referred Freddy to the drug counselors in the drug court program for an assessment. Freddy agreed to go to the appointment for an evaluation.

A few days later, a paralegal for Bob Tucker called to see how Freddy's admission to drug court was going. Mitch mentioned that Freddy probably would not be admitted: Freddy had denied any drug problem and any drug use at all, and defendants charged with distributing drugs were prohibited from entering the program. Bob Tucker called a few days later after the conversation between Mitch and the paralegal. The attorney was upset and wanted to know why Mitch refused to accept Freddy into the program. Mitch repeatedly explained that Freddy had denied any drug use and the distribution charge would make him ineligible for the program. Bob Tucker said he would talk to the prosecutor to have the charge reduced to Possession with Intent to Distribute, which would eliminate the distribution charge. Applicants with PWID charges were routinely accepted in Urban County's drug court.

A week later, Mitch received a fax from the treatment providers, Jane and Kent. Freddy did have a marginal drug problem, with alcohol and ecstasy being the primary drugs of choice. Freddy was vague about his drug use but maintained that he used ecstasy only recreationally. Freddy admitted to Jane that he broke into a lot of cars as a teen. Jane saw him as a real criminal. Having a bad feeling about Freddy, Mitch told Jane that he could see Freddy getting into the program but with very little chance of graduation.

Mitch called Bob Tucker, telling him that Freddy had been assessed and was qualified for the program. However, he believed that Freddy had little chance of graduation. Freddy's lack of motivation, sole focus on clearing his record and vagueness about his drug use were all bad signs, Mitch told Bob Tucker. The attorney told Mitch that he would talk to Freddy about his lackadaisical attitude.

Mitch heard nothing from Freddy for three weeks. In late November, Freddy called and set an appointment to meet with Mitch. A week later,

Mitch told Freddy that he was concerned about his level of motivation to change. Mitch tentatively suggested he might be much more a drug dealer than a user. Freddy claimed that he had thought hard about his situation for a few days and believed that he needed to make a change.

Two days later, Freddy came to Mitch's office to do the final paperwork for admission to drug court. Most importantly, Freddy completed the stipulation to guilt, a written confession and a waiver of some rights related to his drug crimes. Once signed, the document removed all doubt about a conviction if Freddy failed drug court. After the year-end holidays and after Freddy's rescheduling appointments with the counselors for their assessment, Judge Smith admitted Freddy in early March to the program upon Mitch's recommendation. Mitch did not mention his reservation to the judge.[1]

One week later, Mitch learned at the morning staff meeting with the treatment counselors before court was to be held that night that Freddy had tested positive for cocaine. This was his first positive test. In group counseling, Freddy had denied any use and had reported that he had touched some cocaine, which must have been how he had tested positive. Before drug court began that evening, Mitch saw Freddy in the lobby.

"Look, Mr. Solomon, you're a man. You can say what you want, but if you go in there and try to tell me that you tested positive for cocaine because you handled it, that ain't going to fly. I am going to make fun of you," Mitch remarked.

"That isn't what happened," Freddy replied. "I kissed someone that had been using cocaine. That is the only way I can imagine it got into my system."

"You can say what you want, but it just doesn't happen that way."

During court, Mitch called Freddy's case, "Your honor, I would like to call Freddy Solomon. Mr. Solomon tested positive for the presence of cocaine. I will let him explain the exact circumstances."

"I made some wrong decisions, I can see now. I made the decision to hang around the wrong people. Lesson learned."

Judge Smith remarked, "Mr. Solomon, you have been in the program for a week now?"

"Yes, your honor."

"You have heard this all before. I just want to make sure you understand. The first thing is, you see these people around you. You need to

---

1. Despite Mackinem's reservations, other factors influenced the decision to accept Freddy. There was space available; Bob Tucker, a respected attorney, pushed for Freddy's acceptance; and the program tries to help those who meet the admission criteria even when reservations may exist.

work with Mr. Mitch and the counselors. This is very important. You must be truthful with these people. I rely on them. This must become the most important thing in your life right now. You have always heard that your family and your home come first. Those are not first. This is first now. I know you have only been in the program a week, but this is the kind of place where you hit the ground running. There just isn't any kind of lead-time. I will accept the recommendation of the prosecuting attorney and give you 16 hours of community service (which was the standard sanction in this situation)."

In late April, Mitch and the counselors discussed that Freddy was ready to move from Phase 1 of the treatment program to the less intensive Phase 2. Although the treatment staff believed that Freddy saw himself as much better than everyone, they and Mitch decided to recommend the change to the judge. In court, Judge Smith congratulated Freddy on moving to Phase 2 and warned him to "step it up a notch," to continue to make progress. He and the drug court staff did not want Freddy to even consider slipping back a phase.

Despite the staff's ongoing concerns that Freddy seemed to think that he was "better than everyone else," he continued to test clean and attend all his counseling sessions and meetings. In May, upon staff recommendation, the judge moved Freddy to Phase 3.

In July, a problem with Freddy's participation in drug court appeared. The treatment counselor stated in the treatment summary, "Client continues to meet the core group counseling and program requirements, but appears to value his social activities more than his counseling obligations. Recommend the judge challenge Freddy's motivation and lack of effort. Freddy continues to remind all staff that he has attended all sessions and tested clean on all UA's (urine analysis), however does not appear to acknowledge his need for the program. Recommend sanction of 8 hours community service."

Discussion between treatment staff and Mitch revealed even more about Freddy than the note. Kent, a counselor, commented at the morning staffing of the following drug court session that Freddy had never said one substantial thing in the entire weeks he had been coming to counseling. Katie, another counselor, added that he had never discussed his arrest or the drugs. Mitch commented that coming to group counseling and testing clean were what they expected of clients in Phase 1. The staff expected more of clients by Phase 3. Mitch now believed that they had made a mistake in accepting Freddy. Freddy blamed drug court because he couldn't get, as he described it, "a really great job as a drug representative," Kent remarked.

In the pre-court meeting with Judge Smith and the counselors that afternoon, Mitch commented about Freddy to the judge, "This guy has no chance of graduating if he does not get with the program. He thinks staying clean is enough." Kent added that the client was more concerned with his social calendar and when he would graduate. Judge Smith agreed to talk to him.

In court, as Freddy walked down the isle to stand before Judge Smith, Mitch noticed what he was wearing. Freddy wore a loose, casual shirt hanging out of his pants, a baggy pair of shorts, and a pair of sandals. Before Mitch could repeat much of what was said in the pre-court meeting, Judge Smith saw Freddy.

"Don't you ever come here in shorts again," the judge rebuked Freddy. "Do you understand? If you come into my court like that again, I will kick you out."

After the judge's comments about Freddy's attire, Mitch explained that Freddy "had never said one serious thing in group since he had been in the program."

"You better get serious. Do you understand what you need to do?" Judge Smith asked.

Freddy acted surprised, "Now, I know I got a little problem."

"Have a conference with the treatment staff and make sure you exactly understand what it is you need to do," cautioned Judge Smith.

Two weeks later, Mitch asked the counselor, "Does he get it now?" Kent replied, "Yeah, he knows what he has to do, and in the last week he has done well."

"If he could give me a couple of really good weeks, I would get him out, but I can't make it look like he doesn't have to do anything," Mitch commented as the discussion came to a close.

At the next court, Freddy was dressed in slacks, dress shoes and a polo shirt. Mitch told the judge that Freddy had dramatically improved.

The Judge stated, "One look at you, and I can tell things have improved."

In August, during a conference with Libby, a new female counselor, she told Mitch that Freddy had "remarkably improved." She said he was talking more about his future and desire to move on. Despite Libby's claims of a changed Freddy, Mitch had his doubts and believed that Freddy had decided to fake being good. Mitch kept this thought to himself.

In late September, Mitch discussed Freddy with Libby during a staff meeting. She confirmed what she had recently written in her treatment note: Freddy was doing well and seemed to show more effort. He was taking part in his treatment program and was doing better since Phase 1. Libby recommended that the staff plan for Freddy to graduate in the next month. Mitch agreed. While Freddy had not been an outstanding client, he had completed his treatment program; Mitch believed Freddy did his part of the bargain. Mitch felt bound that if a client attended counseling sessions, tested clean and gained staff recommendation for graduation, then the client should graduate despite any doubts.

Before Freddy could graduate, he was rearrested, Mitch heard. Undercover officers had made several buys from his home, eventually catching Freddy with large amounts of heroin and ecstasy in his house. The court sentenced Freddy to serve ten years in prison.

In retrospect it appears that Freddy was a drug dealer and not really an addict. Only in hindsight did Mitch see the warning signs, particularly Freddy's low motivation and lavish lifestyle. Freddy owned a house in a good downtown neighborhood, attended local college football games and went on trips, all without a job.

Through a variety of interrelated activities in various settings, drug court professionals strive to enable drug-using offenders to become drug abstinent and crime free. Sometimes they are successful. Oftentimes they are not, as in Freddy Solomon's participation in drug court. Judges, lawyers, counselors and program coordinators work in courtrooms, in offices, over the phone, in jail, and elsewhere to help drug-using offenders go straight. While the court sessions are the most publicly visible part of drug court, the professionals, except for the drug court judges, do most of their work outside of the courtroom.[2]

In this chapter, we present an overview of the process through which drug court professionals manage drug-using offenders. Our focus is on the process used in Urban County's drug court, though the other two drug courts studied worked within similar processes.[3]

We divide the drug court process into three phases: admission, monitoring, and discharge. We also discuss the professional staff whose work is drug court: prosecutors, program coordinators, defense attorneys, treatment staff and judges. Their professional and organizational philosophies and goals underlie and make understandable their

2. Many works only or primarily focus on the most publicly visible feature of drug courts. In examining only the most public places in drug court, these works cannot address many significant processes and events (Burns & Peyrot, 2003).
3. Nationwide, the legal processes of drug court is likely to vary. Some programs occur while the defendant is on probation and others in lieu of adjudication. Some locations have multiple treatment providers and others have only one. In some programs, the administration of the program occurs before an official court appearance (pre-adjudicatory) or after (post-adjudicatory).

activities. The drug-using men and women who are the applicants and clients of drug court appear in our book through the work of the drug court professionals. Within the drug court process, the drug court professionals make important, subtle, and complex decisions that may enable some drug-using offenders to go straight. Using this chapter as the foundation, the three following chapters take up that complex work.

THE DRUG COURT PROCESS

Through admission, monitoring, and discharge, drug court professionals strive to assist drug-using offenders to go straight. Their goal in admission is to select drug-using offenders who need help and have the potential for doing well in the program. As drug court clients participate in the program, the professionals provide services and monitor the progress of the clients, the latter being our focus. Through monitoring, the staffers evaluate the clients' progress and decide what action to take with the clients, such as punishment or promotion, to help the clients move toward a successful discharge. As clients receive services over many months, the drug court staffers make decisions about the clients' performance and about discharging the clients from the program. Some will graduate; others will be terminated and returned to the jurisdiction of the criminal court.

Admissions

The challenge for the drug court professionals during admissions is to accept applicants who have the potential to do well in the program and are a low risk of hurting the program. In the next chapter, we explore the decision-making process through which staff admit or reject drug court applicants. Here, we present the organizational process through which the admission decision is made. Through *notification of a prospective applicant, setting an appointment, pulling files/filling out forms, interviewing the defendant, requesting input from police and victims, getting an assessment, deliberation*, and *court admission*, drug court professionals admit drug-using offenders into drug court or reject them from it.

The prosecuting attorney's office in Urban County and in other large jurisdictions, constantly had defendants coming and going. At any time between 6,000 and 8,000 defendants were waiting to be prosecuted by the prosecuting attorney's office. These defendants gave rise to 12,000 cases, each charge against a defendant being a case. Many defendants had a drug problem. Nationwide more than 66 percent of all those arrested reported some type of drug use at the time of arrest (Taylor, Fitzgerald, Hunt, Reardon, & Brownstein, 2001). Eighty-three percent of all inmates in federal, state, and local prisons and jails are seriously involved in alcohol and drugs (Belenko, Peugh, & Menedez, 2002). Out of these thousands of cases in Urban County, the drug court program coordinator must locate the potentially worthy applicant. Many more drug-using offenders were appropriate for drug court than became applicants. However, without notification of a prospective applicant, the drug-using offender could not become a client.

When a drug court is established, the program coordinator may need to work for referrals as no reliable source may exist. During the first six months of Urban County's drug court, Mitch reviewed new cases before they were assigned to prosecutors, and he called defense lawyers and visited with public defenders, explaining the new drug court program and requesting referrals. After the first six months, referrals for drug courts occurred without much effort from Mitch. As in Urban County, more referrals for drug court were made than could be accepted in Suburban County once drug court was well established. In Farming County, however, Mitch continued to seek referrals in order to obtain a sufficient number of clients to fill the available treatment slots.[4] When referrals are plentiful, drug court program staff may be more selective in who they accept. When referrals are fewer than can be handled, staff may accept applicants who are evaluated as slightly less worthy of being admitted, perhaps somewhat more risky.

Lawyers for drug-using offenders and family members of the offenders are common individuals who notify drug court coordinators of potential applicants. They were the most common sources of referrals for Mitch in Urban County. In hallway conversations in the courthouse or through phone calls, prosecuting attorneys, public defenders and defense lawyers notified Mitch of potential applicants. Family

---

4. Referrals were difficult to generate because Famrming County's sheriff opposed drug court referrals and the prosecutor was reluctant to override the sheriff's objection. Further, regular prosecutorial court occurred only a few weeks every quarter so the opportunity for referrals from court was limited.

members typically called, asking whether the coordinator could help or could contact the drug-using offender. Defense lawyers and family members might also tell Mitch that the defendants were good people who used drugs and needed a break through participation in drug court. Occasionally, during a probation revocation hearing or other nondrug court session, the presiding judge decided that a defendant was suitable for drug court and had Mitch notified.

Except when the defendant initially contacted the program coordinator about being admitted to drug court, Mitch almost always noted the defendant's name and asked that the defendant directly call him to make an appointment. Family members appeared to be confused. They asked whether they could make the appointment since their drug-using offender was working or otherwise preoccupied. Mitch believed that requiring the defendants to call indicated that they were more motivated to participate in the program than when the family or lawyer set an appointment.

While waiting to be called or after being called to set an appointment, Mitch obtained the defendant's criminal file from the assistant prosecuting attorney. All cases had a file. Defendants were called "cases" by prosecutors and defense attorneys. A copy of incident reports, warrants, police documents, and a variety of internal documents for tracking the cases were in the files.

The warrant provided a brief description of the crime; the defendant's name, birth date, social security number, residential address, and phone number; the prosecuting attorney; and the offense. When Mitch or other drug court coordinators looked at the file, they may have seen information such as a charge for a violent crime or an extensive or violent history of crime that excluded the defendant from drug court.

The following is a modified description about the crime alleged to have been committed by an applicant to Urban County's drug court:

> The defendant was found to be in possession of a quantity of a white powder substance, which is believed to be and field-tested positive for the illegal drug cocaine. This incident occurred at 5050 Mockingbird Lane, in the city limits of Urban City.

When program coordinators meet the defendant for the first time, they gather additional information as they continue to evaluate the defendant's suitability for drug court. Defendants have the opportunity to present themselves as worthy applicants for drug court. Mitch met defendants in jail or at his office. If he met the defendant in jail, the offender was typically represented by a public defender. Mitch and the public defender met together the defendant or "client," as referred to by public defenders. Defendants often were unaware of the pending meeting as indicated by their being asleep or broadly curious when Mitch arrived. For office visits, the defendants have an opportunity to plan how they will present themselves, including what clothes they will wear. While their lawyers seldom accompanied the defendants on office visits to Mitch, family members or significant others did.

During the interviews in the jail or in the coordinator's office, the coordinator fills out various forms including the "processing sheet." During these interviews, Mitch collected a variety of biographical information, both mundane and unique. On the processing sheet, Mitch noted any drug-court relevant information such as the criminal and drug history of the defendant, current charges, age, race, gender, the arresting police department, and victim information. Much of this information was collected for federal reporting purposes as well as simple client identification. Mitch often wrote notes to himself on the form about unique aspects of the applicant such as "used to be a banker" or "home looks unstable."

In the following condensed and reworked passage, Mitch has interviewed in jail a drug offender who had been referred by his public defender. Because Mitch was interviewing inmates that day, the interview with this offender was shorter than the usual forty-five minutes to one hour office interview. After describing the program, Mitch began questioning the offender.

> "OK, then I need to get some information. Tyrone, what will be your address?"
>
> Tyrone answered, "6811 Doby Dr."
>
> "Whose house is that?"
>
> "My mother's house" replied Tyrone, a common answer in Mitch's experience.
>
> "How old is your mother"
>
> "She is 57."
>
> "She's a Christian woman?" Mitch asked. In his experience, Mitch believed that a religious mother can sometimes have a positive effect.
>
> Tyrone answered sternly, "Strictly by the books."

Mitch liked that answer because he believed that a strict Christian woman would provide good support and guidance for Tyrone. Mitch continued, asking the inmate about phone numbers and the availability of transportation, which was important so that the drug court client could attend all the required meetings.

"I have plenty (of) ways to get to the meetings. I am in the bus route. I have plenty of friends to take me to the meetings," reassured Tyrone.

"Which drug do you have a problem with," asked Mitch.

"Crack cocaine," Tyrone replied in a firm voice.

"How often do you use it?"

"I was using it everyday. Every minute, second, and hour."

Caught off guard by the bluntness of the reply, Mitch responded, "That's one of those questions I always ask and one of those questions where I always wonder how much bullshit someone is giving me. Somebody says, 'Oh, I have a problem with crack cocaine, and I use it about once a week.'"

Tyrone interjected, "There's no such thing. Every day, 24 hours a day!"

After asking the inmate about other drugs he abused, Mitch learned that the inmate had gone to three residential treatment programs. Continuing, Mitch asked, "How long were you sober?"

"The longest I stayed clean was about 2 years."

After learning that Tyrone was unemployed and hopeful of getting a job when released, Mitch asked, "Alright. Anything else I should let the judge know?"

"No, that's about it, besides my parole time."

Worried that this might be a potential problem, Mitch asked, "OK, what are you on parole for?"

Tyrone answered, "I am on parole for distribution."

Knowing that a charge for distributing drugs would not ban him from the program, Mitch thanked the inmate for his time.

During all the application interviews, Mitch learned of unique biographical information of the drug offenders and gathered routine bureaucratic information about them.

Before sending the applicant to see treatment counselors for an assessment and after the file had been pulled, Mitch sent letters to the arresting officer and to any victim, requesting their judgment about the defendant's admission into drug court. Mitch considered the response of the police officer in deciding whether to admit the applicant, but the officer did not have a veto over the decision. The victim, however, did have a veto over the admission, as directed by the prosecuting attorney.[5] That rarely happened. Corporate victims did not have a veto, in part, because corporate policies often routinely deny any diversion of criminal cases.

The letter to the officer explained the rigors of the drug court program such as three counseling sessions per week and drug screening every week; noted that the defendant must stipulate to guilt to be admitted and, therefore, could be quickly and successfully prosecuted should the defendant drop out; and mentioned that the drug court program is less effective with those who are serious drug sellers compared to those who are drug users and less effective with those who have no desire to change. Whenever officers characterized a defendant as a dealer and therefore should be denied admission, Mitch considered seriously the officer's judgment. Some letters were not returned and, if not returned by the arresting officer, were taken to indicate no objection. Some officers rejected the defendant; some supported acceptance. Occasionally, officers commented that they thought the defendant would do well in the program.

As the program coordinator, Mitch believed it was important for the treatment staff to assess the drug court applicant. To applicants not in jail, Mitch gave the names and phone number of the treatment staff. He told the applicants to call and set their own appointment and to call him after meeting with the treatment counselors. This meeting provided the counselors the opportunity to learn about the applicants and participate in the admission decision.

Applicants in jail who Mitch decided were to be recommended for admission to drug court were seen by the treatment staff in a holding cell, called "the hole" in Urban County's courthouse, shortly before they went before the judge, who officially admitted them into drug court. These eight-foot square cells had a small toilet and wash basin and graffiti on their walls, sometimes graffiti about drug court or Mitch. Across two-sided counters separated by a metal screen, the drug court applicant and the treatment staff met briefly. Compared to the arrangements in Suburban County and Farming County where drug court applicants (and other defendants to appear in court) were handcuffed and left in the courtroom until court began, "the hole" was accommodating.

---

5. Mackinem recalls several attorneys who were chastised by the Chief Prosecuting Attorney when victims complained about their treatment. Victims were very important to the Chief Prosecuting Attorney, which may be related to his elective position.

As Mitch learned about the drug court applicant through reviewing the file, talking with the defendant, receiving information from the arresting officer, talking to the treatment staff, and in other ways, he deliberated about whether to recommend to the judge that the applicant be admitted into drug court. As Mitch deliberated, he may have decided to reject the applicant and considered the reasons for doing so, such as the applicant's experiencing a serious mental health condition beyond the capabilities of the program to serve. Mitch explained the rejection when the drug court applicant saw him after meeting with the treatment staff if the rejection did not occur before that meeting. Mitch may have had concerns such as whether the applicant was sufficiently motivated to participate effectively in drug court, whether the criminal charge disqualified the applicant from participation, or whether the applicant was sufficiently emotionally stable to participate. When Mitch experienced concerns, he discussed these matters with the relevant professional staff before making a decision to recommend or reject the applicant.

When Mitch provisionally accepted the applicant, he set up a drug court appearance for the applicant to be officially admitted into the program by the judge. Before the court appearance, Mitch saw the provisionally accepted drug court client at which time the client signed a "Basic Understanding" of the rules and sanctions of the program and filled out the stipulation of guilt, a legal confession to the crime for which the defendant had been charged. This stipulation of guilt became a tool for the drug court staff to coerce the drug court client's compliance with the program.

The drug court judge officially admitted the drug court applicant into the program during the public court session of drug court. Mitch, as well as the program coordinator in Suburban County's drug court, called the provisionally accepted drug court client to stand before the judge and briefly commented on the applicant's drug situation. After asking a few questions of and receiving sensible responses from the drug court applicant, perhaps about whether the defendant had a drug problem and where the defendant worked, the judge welcomed the applicant into the drug court program. For those entering the program from jail, the judge filled out a bond form authorizing their release the next morning. That night after their release, they were required to go to group counseling.

Monitoring

Once drug-using offenders became drug court clients, the professional staff provided services and monitored their progress. The staff decided what actions to take such as promoting a client into a more advanced phase of the program or sanctioning the client for violation of program requirements such as testing positive for drug use. Our work focuses on the monitoring and decision making, not the provision of services. In Chapter 4, we explore the interaction among the staff and their decision making as they monitored the drug court clients' progress in the program. Here, we present an overview of the monitoring process.

Briefly, drug court clients participated in drug court through attending group and individual counseling sessions and community self-help meetings, submitting to drug tests, and paying fees. Every two weeks they went before the judge in drug court to have their progress reviewed and sanctions provided for their successes or failures in following the requirements of the program. When clients had violated program requirements, the conversations between them and the professional staff, including the judge, could be contentious. In Urban County's drug court, clients typically attended group counseling two or three times each week. When a severe or ongoing problem occurred with drug court clients such as repeated positive tests for drugs or missed meetings, clients may have received individual counseling. Drug court clients were required to attend at least two self-help meetings each week, such as Alcoholics Anonymous or Narcotics Anonymous.

Drug testing was a critical component of drug court. Through a system of phone calls and color codes, drug court clients were tested randomly throughout the week. The system was difficult to anticipate, and Mitch believed that it kept the clients on edge about using drugs.

During a typical week in Urban County's drug court program, a client might go to group counseling at 6:00 P.M. on Monday, Wednesday and Thursday. Before the start of one of these sessions, the client would be required to urinate in a cup and have it tested for drugs. On Saturday or Sunday, the client would attend a self-help meeting. Perhaps one night after group counseling, the client would go to a self-help meeting with some other clients. Once a month, the client might leave work early to meet with the client's counselor in an individual session.

Clients were required to pay fees to the treatment providers. By paying these fees, the client contributed to the overall cost of the services. The drug court program paid the balance of the costs.

As clients participated in the drug court program, the professional staff monitored their behavior, evaluated their progress, and decided what to do with the clients, including whether to promote them in the program or sanction them for violating program requirements such as testing "dirty" for drug use. Treatment staff and program coordinators wrote case notes to document the monitoring, evaluation, and decisions concerning the clients' participation in the program.

The drug court professionals discussed the clients' participation in the program and decided what would be done with the clients. These discussions were held in regularly scheduled staff meetings between the treatment counselors and the program coordinator, which ran from thirty minutes to two hours and were typically held in the morning or the early evening when the court sessions were held for drug court in Urban County. There were unscheduled telephone calls and other conversations between the counselors and the coordinator, which usually concerned a current problem or a potential problem. In addition, pre-court meetings of the judge, counselors, coordinator, and lawyers were reviewed, including the public court sessions.

In the following staffing between Mitch, the program coordinator, and Jane, Calvin and Katie, treatment counselors for the treatment provider for Urban County drug court, they discussed the counselors' recommendation that Jerome, a client who eventually was removed from the program, be sent to Green Village, a local state-run residential treatment program for drug abusers. As Mitch told it:

> At 10:00 A.M. I went over to New Start (the treatment provider). When I entered the office, I found Jane sitting at the computer putting the finishing comments on the staffing notes.
>
> "This is a bad sign; you must not be done yet?"
>
> "Almost," she cheerfully replied.
>
> I hung out and said "hi" to Katie and Calvin. By then, Jane had finished the notes and was making copies for the meeting. Jane handed me a copy of the notes, and I sat down to read them in her office. After reading the notes, I commented, "It seems pretty clear to me. Who do we need to discuss?" I remarked that Adam is out without comment from anyone, Jim S. quit, and Paul has disappeared.

The staff wanted to discuss Jerome. Jerome is a large male with a gang background. He was doing very well in the program but had been in trouble lately. Calvin reported that Jerome was attacked by members of his former gang. Subsequently, he used Tylox (a narcotic drug) and cocaine, which he later reported in the group. Calvin seemed quite worried about it. The treatment staff's recommendation was for Jerome to be sent to jail until he could be admitted to Green Village. I expressed concern.

"Why jail," I asked.

Calvin explained, "It may be the only way for him to not get killed by these guys. It worked last time. The weekend gave him time to chill out and not be found out."

"I don't mind, but if we are doing it for his own good, then I would like for this to be discussed with him," I replied.

We discussed this suggestion, and, finally, I suggested to Calvin, "You talk to him and then let me know what you want to do. Are you alright with that?" That suited Calvin.

In the pre-court meeting held immediately before the court session (which were held every two weeks in Urban County) the judge, lawyers, treatment staff and program coordinator briefly discussed the clients. Mitch wrote a one-line summary about each client for the judge. He was prepared to say much more in the meeting and in court. For example, if a client was progressing without any problems, he wrote "OK." If the client had tested positive on a drug test for cocaine, he wrote "+ for cocaine." As the judge asked about the clients, the coordinator and treatment staff provided information about the clients' recent progress. They also made recommendations for sanctioning those clients who had violated program requirements. Frequently, the treatment staff, coordinator and lawyers discussed the clients and the recommendations. While the judge typically agreed with the recommendations, he (the judges were male in the courts we studied) would occasionally comment that he would wait for the court session with the clients to decide what to do.[6]

In the public court session, the judge responded with praise or punishment to the client's behavior as reported by the coordinator. In Urban County's drug court, Mitch first presented to the judge clients with "problems," then clients whose progress was satisfactory, and

6. While the state's Chief Justice is a woman, the overwhelming majority of judges are male both in trial courts and in drug courts. Of the 51 trial judges in the state, four are women.

finally clients who were graduating from the program. This order allowed the court session to end positively. Suburban County's and Farming County's drug courts used different orders for presenting clients.[7]

Sanctions for rule violations were part of the judge's duties and were an important element of the program. Based on the recommendations of the coordinator and treatment staff and based on the responses of the drug court clients to the judge's questioning, the judge imposed sanctions that ranged from several hours of community service to confinement in jail for a couple of days. In Urban County's drug court, the requirements included obeying all laws and probation conditions; reporting any violations, arrests or charges within twenty-four hours, including any driving or minor violations; not using any alcohol or drugs and if use occurred, immediately informing the counselor; attending all drug court sessions and treatment sessions; making satisfactory progress; paying restitution where required; paying a participation fee of $20 per week; and notifying the program coordinator within forty-eight hours of any change of residence, change in telephone number or service, and any other important information used to stay in contact with the program.

Appearances before the judge and the judge's sanctioning had become routine in the three drug courts we studied, especially in Suburban County's court. Drug court clients spent less than one minute before the judge in Suburban County when Mitch observed. A client who was progressing satisfactorily stood before the judge for as little as ten seconds. While clients who had violated requirements of the program could stand before the judge for many minutes, often their review and sanctioning took about fifteen seconds in Suburban County's drug court. The review and sanctioning discussion took place in the pre-court meetings.

Discharge

Drug court staff discharged clients from the program in three ways. The complexity of discharging clients is taken up in Chapter 5. Clients

7. In Suburban County's drug court the clients were presented by phases, phase 1 went first and so on. Within phases, the clients were present in alphabetical order. Farming County's court was small. The treatment provider's report was formatted alphabetically and, during the early years of observation, the clients were presented alphabetically. Later, the presentation went very much like the Urban County model.

who quit the program through failing to appear were terminated. They had "disappeared." Staff rarely knew why clients had disappeared. Occasionally, staff members remarked after the clients failed to appear that they saw the disappearances coming, but Mitch had his doubts about his colleagues' prescience. Many months later, staff members may hear a story from a graduate of drug court or a police officer about what happened to the client.

Consider Mark, a client who was married with three children, who disappeared from drug court. He and his wife were addicted to heroin. While Mark was trying to quit, his wife was not a client anywhere and saw no reason to quit her drug use. Mark often discussed with the counselors his fear that his wife would take the kids and abandon him because she was not willing to try to quit using drugs. A few weeks after Mark failed to appear for counseling, a story began to circulate among staff and clients that his wife used the threat of taking their children to coerce him to leave with her for the West. One client reported that a friend had seen Mark entering a van with his wife immediately after he failed to appear for counseling.

Program staff, with the judge making the final decision, removed clients who failed to progress satisfactorily and returned them to the jurisdiction of the criminal court. Removal was common for clients who were arrested on new charges, but not automatic. "Kicking out a client," as staff often called removing a client, required staff review, planning and action that resulted in termination.

Graduation, a joyous court occasion with speeches, certificates, and even receptions, was a successful discharge from the program. Staff's review and preparation preceded graduation, which resulted in the removal of all legal obligations for the charges to which the drug court clients stipulated their guilt. Often, weeks before the graduation, staff members informed clients that they were moving toward graduation. In the court session preceding graduation, staff and the judge told clients of their upcoming discharge. Through admission, monitoring and discharge, drug court professionals strove to enable drug-using offenders to go straight. Graduation was the successful result of the drug court process.

THE PROFESSIONAL STAFF

The professional staff of drug court is composed of long-time court professionals and those who are newer to courts. Judges and defense and prosecuting attorneys have been crucial professionals in courts. Program coordinators and treatment counselors are newer members of the court team, and team is how drug court staff members understand themselves. Through the coercive powers of the court and the treatment and interest of the staff and judge, they work together to reduce crime by helping drug-using offenders become abstinent, law-abiding citizens.

The drug court professionals work within the culture and organization of the local criminal court (Flemming, Nardulli, & Eisenstein, 1992). The work of law is a craft. It depends less on a sharp legal mind than on interpersonal skills and judgment that lawyers develop through experience. The courthouse can be understood as a community of professional participants bound together by their interdependence in managing criminal cases (Flemming et al., 1992). Through repeated interactions and through the unplanned and often unnoticed importation into court of the larger societal pattern of relations among people, drug court professionals structure relations among themselves and the other participants. Every case is a "complex structure of social positions and relationships" (Black, 1989). For example, when a defense attorney who is well known and respected by the coordinator refers a drug-using offender to the coordinator, the program coordinator is likely to be favorably disposed toward the offender. Freddy Solomon's attorney, Bob Tucker, was able to expedite his client's admission into drug court because of his prominence and experience with the prosecutors and the program coordinator.

Finally, the drug court, like any court, is shaped by local politics, though not controlled by local politics (Ulmer & Kramer, 1998). For example, another city in the southeastern state where our three courts are located is known to be quite conservative. That city's drug court requires that its participants plead guilty before they are admitted. Having funding for a drug court and needing no support from the local bar or public defender's office, the prosecuting attorney in this more conservative city was able to establish the drug court as a post-plea program despite the resistance of public defenders. In post-plea drug courts, defendants enter a guilty plea before a judge in a traditional public court hearing. Other drug courts do not require a guilty plea.[8]

Drug courts operate within, as well as modify and extend, the culture and social structure of the local courthouse, which itself responds to the local political culture. Prosecutors, program coordinators, defense lawyers, treatment staff and judges are the professional staff members who operate drug court. In order, we briefly discuss each of these professionals' orientations toward drug court.

Prosecutors

Prosecuting attorneys, who were the chief prosecutors in our southeastern state, were locally elected officials. Assistant prosecuting attorneys prosecuted cases. As program coordinator, Mitch worked for the prosecuting attorney. While assistant prosecuting attorneys did not have a veto over who was admitted to drug court in Urban County, without their support, admitting a drug-using offender became much more difficult. While drug courts were not a primary concern for assistant prosecuting attorneys, the drug courts were congruent as well as incongruent with the assistant prosecuting attorneys' orientation to prosecution.

Assistant prosecuting attorneys referred cases to drug court. While occasionally the assistant prosecuting attorneys expressed reservations about admitting an applicant to the program, after discussion with the program coordinator, the assistant prosecuting attorneys in all three courts we studied typically were willing to allow the admission.

The primary expectation for assistant prosecuting attorneys was to "move the case." Cases where defendants were still in jail after ninety days automatically came to the attention of the chief administrator for the prosecuting attorney's office in both jurisdictions in which our three drug courts were located. Assistant prosecuting attorneys received a list of their ninety-day cases and met monthly with the prosecuting attorney to discuss what they planned to do with these cases. Assistant prosecuting attorneys might be demoted for failing to satisfactorily move the cases.

Assistant prosecuting attorneys use discretion to help them move cases (Hawkins, 1992). Based on various elements of the case, they

8. The guilty plea before the judge is a final and nearly irrevocable act. All that remains is the punishment. Any legal act before the plea is less final.

may decide to dismiss a case when they believe the chance of obtaining a guilty verdict is remote (Frohmann, 1991; Spohn et al., 2001). They may also try to plea bargain the case, trading less severe punishments for a plea of guilty (McConville & Mirsky, 1995; McCoy, 1993).

Assistant prosecuting attorneys view cases according to their convictability and seriousness among other considerations. Some cases are "dead-bang guilty," where the defendant is seen as absolutely guilty and no problem with the prosecution of the defendant exists. Other cases have reasonable doubt; the defendant has been overcharged or other problems exist with the evidence. Some cases are understood to be serious due to the type of crime, the previous record of the offender and perhaps the age at which the offender first offended (Mather, 1979). Prosecutors may view a case where the defendant has a history of drug use even if the offense does not involve drugs as a drug court case, as a serious case, as one to go to trial or as a case to be pled. Drug court cases were the dead-bang guilty cases.

Assistant prosecuting attorneys in the courts we studied typically did not initiate the referral of a case to drug court. As one assistant prosecuting attorney in Farming County's court commented to Mitch:

> I have never made a referral on my own. I guess I am not much of a self-starter. It always comes because the public defender suggested it. I wish it would happen more often. I mean if it were the root cause of them being here, I would rather they (i.e., drug court) take care of it. It is a problem because it seems to stay on my docket forever, but screw the docket. It is better they (i.e., drug court) take care of their (i.e., the offenders') problem.

When the defendants, family members or defense lawyers mentioned that the defendants had a drug problem, the assistant prosecuting attorneys considered or agreed to a referral of the defendants to drug court. Few of the assistant prosecuting attorneys in Urban County knew well the admission criteria to drug court, but they trusted Mitch to review the cases and make certain that the defendants were appropriate for drug court.

Assistant prosecuting attorneys appeared willing to send cases to drug court when they believed that the defendants would receive some help with their drug problem. They were willing even though the several weeks or longer that it may have taken to admit a defendant to drug court, including the opening of available treatment slots in the program, interfered with the "move-the-case" orientation of the assistant prosecuting attorneys. Once the case had been admitted to drug court, it had been "moved" off the active docket of the assistant prosecuting attorneys.

Program Coordinators

Program coordinators, also known as directors or managers, are in charge of the day-to-day operation of drug court. They are likely to be the only drug court professionals whose full-time responsibilities involve drug court. Drug court coordinators are a new addition to the courthouse scene. The professional background, office location, and the employer of the coordinator vary in drug courts throughout the United States and other countries (Goldkamp et al., 2001). Coordinators typically have a legal or treatment background. They may be positioned within the legal system or outside of it. For example, Mitch had many years of experience as a drug counselor, was employed by the prosecuting attorney, and had his office in Urban County's courthouse. In Lexington, Kentucky, a recent coordinator also had a treatment background but was employed by a community service center and was located outside the courthouse. In one New Mexico drug court, a local county government employed a former probation agent as the program coordinator. In Suburban County's drug court, the original treatment coordinator, Carl, was a lawyer employed by the prosecuting attorney and located in the courthouse.

Program coordinators are gatekeepers. They decide which drug-using offenders who come to their attention to reject or to recommend to the judge to be admitted. Program coordinators know that admitting a defendant into drug court can help move the prosecutors' cases, though drug court failures disrupt the docket of cases as those defendants become again the responsibility of the assistant prosecuting attorneys. Successful clients validate the existence of drug court. Unsuccessful cases, especially where new crimes are committed, could harm the program as well as the public.

In addition to keeping the gate, program coordinators explain drug court to a large number and variety of people. Mitch received or made more than twenty-five phone calls each day. He met with defendants, family members or lawyers several times each day. He explained to the arresting officer what would happen if the defendant failed the program. He explained to family members why their drug-using member would not be admitted. He explained to lawyers who would be a good candidate for drug court. In all these and more explanations, Mitch was educating others about drug court, perhaps persuading them about a course of action, or doing some of each.

Defense Attorneys

Whether private attorneys or public defenders, defense attorneys often initiate the movement of defendants from routine criminal prosecution to drug court. Private attorneys, whether high-priced and powerful or less costly and less influential, are paid by defendants or their representatives to provide good legal service. Mitch often knew the latter, mid-priced attorneys, who made efforts to facilitate the admission of their clients into drug court. For example, one private attorney contacted Mitch every day for a week to help her client enter the program.

Public defenders referred more drug offenders to drug court than did private defense attorneys. Due to the low pay (approximately $30,000 for beginning public defenders in the courts we studied) and the large number of cases to handle (150 to 200 at any one time was not unusual according to public defenders we interviewed), public defenders frequently left after a few years and were not able to focus on serving their clients to the extent that private attorneys could.

Public defenders referred defendants to drug court for two primary reasons: to move the case and to help the defendants. Public defenders felt similar pressure as did assistant prosecuting attorneys to move cases off the docket. They also experienced satisfaction in helping drug-using offenders get help and go straight. As one public defender commented to Mitch, "There are two things a PD (i.e., public defender) looks for. First, how can I get this guy out of jail and, second, how can I help him? Drug court does both of those things. As a PD, I get to see them (i.e., the defendants) again and again."

In the early days of the Urban County drug court, public defenders were concerned that drug court, with its stipulation of guilt, denied clients the opportunity to defend themselves. It became clear, however, that defendable cases that were also appropriate for drug court were rare. One attorney told Mitch, "They're (i.e., the defendants are) guilty. The only question is what to do with them." Nationwide, more than 95 percent of cases are resolved through plea bargaining, an indication, though not a perfect one, of the high percentage of dead-bang guilty cases, cases which public defenders must move quickly (Durose & Langan, 2003; Mather, 1979).

Public defenders and private defense attorneys experienced satisfaction in seeing their clients go straight and improve their lives. The downside was the anguish when clients made their lives worse by failing drug court. Public defenders many times cursed or expressed regret when Mitch told them that their clients had tested positive for drug use or had failed the program. Several attorneys kept a tally of how many clients graduated and how many failed.

Defense attorneys said (in talking with Mitch) that they referred defendants to drug court who were motivated to change, who "rang true" from their experience. Beyond this, we cannot say how defense attorneys decided who to refer. But once defendants were in the program, the defense attorneys became part of the drug court team. Mitch told the attorneys that they were to defend their clients' rights and make sure that the actions taken in court were legal. Occasionally, defense attorneys pointed out questionable legal matters, such as comments about a client overheard by another client and repeated by a third client were hearsay and could not be considered by the court as evidence of the first clients' misdeeds. More frequently, defense attorneys made recommendations to the judge as to what should be done with the drug court clients, advocated for the clients, and provided interpretations of the clients' behavior. However, in Farming County, where public defenders were part-time employees, they never attended drug court.

TREATMENT STAFF

While treatment counselors participated in the admission phase of drug court, they were most involved during the monitoring of the clients as they counseled and drug tested the clients. When Mitch referred drug court applicants to treatment staff for an assessment, the counselors reviewed all available clinical information about the applicants' living arrangements, social relations, drug use, physical health, and mental health. They performed a biopsychosocial assessment, which typically took one and a half hours. From this assessment, the treatment counselors gave Mitch their judgment as to the appropriateness of the applicant for drug court. If they had concerns or objections, the staff might also tell the judge of those in pre-court meetings. Only a few times did the treatment staff flatly reject an applicant. One such rejection occurred when a young woman, charged with PWID cocaine, was also on a series of medications for her panic disorder. The counselor commented that the staff would never know if the young woman was clean since she was taking Xanex, a prescription muscle relaxant.

Treatment staffers varied by gender, age, race, educational attainment, years of experience, and whether they were recovering drug users or nonusers. In Urban County's drug court, Mitch contracted with several treatment providers whose counselors varied widely.[9] They also used different treatment approaches and philosophies.

One of the original treatment programs for Urban County's drug court program was an outpatient therapeutic community. The outpatient therapeutic model, which was a local invention, followed the therapeutic community model that stresses confrontation, 12-step principles, and aggressive staff actions (Tims et al., 1994; Weppner, 1983). The treatment program that provided the bulk of services in all three courts during our study was a "criminal-thinking" program (Samenow, 1984; Yochelson & Samenow, 1976). The criminal-thinking model, also called the cognitive model, emphasizes that criminal action and addiction are based on thinking errors on the part of the defendant. Treatment aims to teach the drug court client new cognitive patterns.

Treatment counselors were most intensely involved with the drug court clients during the provision of services to the clients and the monitoring of their behavior. Similarly, during this phase of the drug court process, counselors were the professionals with whom the clients had the most contact. In addition to counseling and drug testing the clients, the counselors wrote notes and summaries of the counseling sessions, managed crises, collected fees, and set counseling appointments. Through them, the program coordinator, lawyers, and the judge learned of the clients' participation in drug court.

9. Interestingly, we could find no information profiling the composition of the counselors working with drug court; whereas the composition for the clients is readily available and frequently updated.

Beliefs about Drug Addiction, Treatment, and Testing

Based on their beliefs about drug addiction, treatment and testing, drug court counselors (and program coordinators) worked with and evaluated the clients' participation in drug court. We discuss each in turn.

First, counselors and coordinators in all three drug courts we studied and throughout the country typically understand addiction to be a compulsive behavior disorder where the individual continues to use the substance despite significantly negative social, psychological, legal and financial consequences. Whether it is useful to describe addiction as a disease, clearly, the "disease concept" is the dominant paradigm today (Jellinek, 1960; Peele, 1989).

Second, the compulsion to use is regarded as a product of biological, psychological and social drives (Jellinek, 1960; Lobdell, 2004). Biologically, the compulsion may be generated by the drug user's desire to avoid the painful symptoms of withdrawal. Childhood traumas, emotional conflicts, shame, and guilt are a few of the psychological conditions that may propel a person to use. Cognitive styles may also promote the use of illicit substances (Yochelson & Samenow, 1976). For example, if a person has limited means-ends reasoning, the individual is more likely to commit a crime. Peer associations and membership in a drug using subculture or network will socially promote the continued substance use. All three dimensions to varying degrees compel the individual to continue using mood-altering substances despite significant and reoccurring negative consequences.

Third, counselors believe that due to the biological changes created by the substance and the psychological accommodations associated with use, drug users cannot easily assess and evaluate their condition. Drug users lie to themselves and to those around them, often called denial. Denial is not static. Drug users may have startling clarity into their problems at times, but not see the most obvious aspects of their lives at other times.

Treatment attempts to change the drug user on biological, psychological, and social levels (NIDA, 2000; White, 1998). Treating an addiction is a process and not an event. The treatment intensity varies with the individual's progress. The services are divided into phases based upon client progress, program length and number of phases. The drug court programs we studied varied for the majority of clients from one year of services to almost two years. All three programs used three phases. In Phase 1, the most intense, clients spent nine to twelve hours in counseling per week. In Phase 3, clients spent two hours in counseling every other week. Phase 1 was the most intense, because the clients were most likely to have trouble with program compliance and drug use abstinence. Phase 1 commonly lasted three to five months in a year-long program. By the time a client moved to Phase 3, staff expected clients to comply with all program rules and to make substantial progress toward stable abstinence.

The process of moving toward abstinence, called recovery, is characterized by periods of illicit drug use, termed relapses. In the early stages of counseling, the staff and other group members seek to "break through" the denial and enable the drug users to define themselves as addicts. Once drug users come to accept the addict identity, the counseling moves to teaching the clients skills and techniques for avoiding future drug use (McIntosh & McKeganey, 2000). Counselors commonly referred to these as "tools." Tools are the capabilities to handle the desire to do drugs when that desire appears. Tools will include the activities and verbal skills needed to manage emotional upsets created by normal life, from such basics as learning to share intimacy, to discussing childhood trauma, to the more existential accepting "life on life's terms." Tools may also include learning new cognitive skills (Kadden et al., 1995).

Treatment seeks to return addicted individuals to physical health and change their thinking about themselves and their use of mood-altering substances. Finally, treatment will seek to change the clients' social networks. Treatment staff push clients to avoid all former drug-using friends and associates, commonly called changing "playmates and playgrounds" (Anonymous, 2001).

Counselors and other professional staff expect specific client behaviors. First, addicts lie about drug use. Lying helps avoid stigma and promotes continued use (Furst, Johnson, Dunlap, & Curtis, 1999). Second, clients make bad decisions. When clients skip meetings, seek medical care, or go out Friday night, staff assumes clients are seeking drugs. Being late for a group counseling session could be a simple mistake or a sign that the client is returning to drug use. Third, despite the staff's best effort, clients are likely to relapse while in the program. Termed by staff as a "simple slip" or a "full-blown relapse," returning to illicit drug use is a normal part of the recovery process. Fourth, clients must change. Relapses and bad decisions are expected when clients first enter drug treatment. After sufficient time, staff expects no additional relapses.

Counselors and other staff understand drug testing to be a critical component of drug court. Drug testing is necessary to catch clients using drugs (Borg, 2000; DeJong & Wish, 2000; Knudsen, Roman, & Johnson, 2004; Yacoubian, 2000). In all three drug courts we studied, the staff fully trusted the drug-testing results. Never did staff openly doubt the test. The science of drug testing supports such confidence. For example, neither second-hand smoke nor holding cocaine will result in a positive test (Hawks & Chiang, 1986). However, counselors' beliefs about how to interpret drug test results were not always supported by the drug test manufacturers or by the technology of drug testing (Mackinem & Higgins, 2007). We discuss how counselors interpreted drug test results in Chapter 4 when we examine how counselors and other staff responded to clients' explanations for their positive drug tests. Within these beliefs and expectations about drug addiction, treatment and testing, counselors and other staff worked with and evaluated clients' participation in drug court, including clients' violations of program requirements such as abstaining from drugs.

JUDGES

Judges have the ultimate authority in drug court, but they often depend heavily, and wisely so, on the judgments of the coordinators and counselors. Research has shown that the judge's supervision and comments are central to drug court success (Marlowe, Festinger, & Lee, 2004; Marlowe, Festinger, Lee, & Dugosh, 2006). Drug court judges are expected to be fair and impartial arbitrators between the various and competing entities in the court. According to the National Association of Drug Court Professionals (NADCP, 1999), the judge must do so in spite of contractual obligations, collaborative ethos and personal relationships (Freeman-Wilson, Tuttle, & Weinstein, 2001). Based on Mitch's national experiences, it appears that most drug court judges are county based. They may be elected or appointed in a specific jurisdiction. They often have broad political support and influence in the jurisdiction over which they preside. As a result, judges often lead the effort for the establishment of drug court.

In the southeastern state in which we studied drug court, the drug court judges were typically circuit judges with primary duties other than drug court. Circuit judges were selected by the general assembly and, as in colonial days, "rode the circuit." Judges were routinely assigned for six months out of the year to a circuit other than their "home" circuit. This posed challenges for drug court.

When judges rotated to another circuit, a new judge needed to be obtained to hold drug court. With judges rotating from circuit to circuit, they had less investment in any particular drug court. They also had less influence with the local law enforcement and a weaker political base in those jurisdictions that were not their home circuit.

Drug court judges in Urban County and Suburban County were circuit judges, with the challenges that circuit judges posed for drug court. In Farming County no circuit judge was readily available. Mitch arranged for a magistrate to become the drug court judge through special authorization from the Chief Justice of the state's Supreme Court. Located in every county, magistrates handled minor crimes and driving infractions. Being a county official and appointed by the local state senator, magistrates were often well connected to local officials.

Nationally, some drug courts are held in lieu of regular criminal court and, therefore, can be held during the day by drug court judges as part of their range of duties. In other drug court programs, court is held in the evening, after normal working hours. This makes it easier for drug court clients to hold jobs. In our southeastern state, drug court judges volunteered for this extra duty, as they did in Urban and Suburban counties, or they oversaw drug court as part of their range of court duties, as in Farming County. All three courts that we studied were held in the evening. Community commitment, belief in drug court, and/or other altruistic motives underlay the volunteering by judges of their time to the drug courts we studied.[10]

At a luncheon speech given by our southeastern state's first drug court judge during a statewide drug court conference (one of many speeches that he gave about drug court), Judge Callahan provided insight about the reasons that some judges are willing to volunteer for drug court:

---

10. Mitch's experience with drug court judges from other states indicate the same motives for judges in other states who volunteer their services to drug court as for the judges whose three drug courts we studied.

"I'm not saying we don't need prisons. We do. I am saying we need to be smarter about how we punish people." The judge then told a story of a murder case over which he had presided. The defendant was a married man who had a serous problem with crack. He had several criminal charges. The defendant had quit crack and had started putting his life back together. The man and his wife were planning a little second honeymoon to celebrate their new life. Before they left, the man went out and got high on crack. After he used all his money, he went home to his wife and demanded more money. When she refused, the man beat her with a nearby mike stand. The stand bent, and the man went and got a stronger one and continued to beat his wife. He went and got a knife and stabbed her more than 50 times. The man turned himself in a few hours later. Standing before the judge, the man said he killed his wife because of the crack.

Judge Callahan continued, telling his audience that he wished that the criminal justice system had been able to reach that man earlier, provide the help that man needed, and save the lives of the wife and the husband. With a tone of regret, Judge Callahan remarked that had drug court existed before the tragedy occurred, it may have been avoided.

Drug court judges have the court authority and ultimate responsibility for deciding what will be done with drug court applicants and clients–who will be admitted, what action will be taken as the client moves through the program, who will be removed from the program and who will graduate. Judges praise and punish drug court clients. In the three courts we studied, the judges relied greatly on the information provided by and the expertise and advice of the program coordinators and treatment counselors and listened to the suggestions and concerns of the lawyers. However, they did not merely rubber stamp the recommendations given to them.[11]

In Urban County's drug court, Mitch discussed the responsibilities of the new drug court judges with them, as in the following:

Judge: "I read this notebook (prepared by Mitch) and I got the basics. As far as sanctions, let me ask you, will you always give a recommendation?"

Mitch: "Yes, sir."

11. The importance of judges in drug courts should not be underestimated. The actions of judges are particularly important in the success of high-risk clients (Marlowe et al., 2004). Drug court participants were randomly assigned to differing intensity levels of judicial supervision. Lower-risk offenders were found to do well with low levels of supervision, whereas high-risk offenders did well only with frequent judicial supervision.

Judge: "At least initially, I am counting on you to lead me the right way."
Mitch: "I will be happy to do that. In all cases, you will get a file like this" (Mitch handed the judge an actual file, and went over some of the forms in the file). "In terms of practical action, I will present the bad cases first. First the jail people (i.e., ones that the judge had decided would very likely go to jail for their infraction), then the people who may go to jail. I save the good ones for last. The reason to do it that way is to free up the deputies early in the process."
Judge: "I see–good thinking ending on a high note."

Drug court judges are the official head of the drug court team of professionals. As they gain experience in drug court, they may increasingly come to exert their independent judgment.

CONCLUSION

Drug court is not a place nor is it a judicial event. Drug court is the working of drug court professionals in interaction with one another as they attempt to help drug-using offenders become abstinent and go straight. We conceptualized the drug court process as occurring through three phases: admission, monitoring and discharge. The drug court professionals engage in this process with one another in various places over months, even years, with any specific drug-using offender. Drug court professionals work within the culture and organization of the local criminal court. The drug court professionals also modify that culture and organization with the introduction of professionals, such as coordinators and counselors, who are not typical participants in the courthouse, and with the use of a therapeutic approach inserted into a jurisprudential system of coercive authority and due-process rights.

Within the drug court process, the drug court professionals make critical, often subtle, and complex decisions in working with drug-using offenders. The offenders are active participants in the drug court process, not passive objects of the professionals' decisions and actions. However, in our writing, the drug-using offenders appear through the work of the professionals, through the professionals' talk, evaluations, interpretations, discussions, decisions and more. In the following three chapters we examine that complex drug court work. First, we turn to the work of judging potential.

Chapter 3

JUDGING POTENTIAL

In late June, Jennifer Johnson, an assistant prosecuting attorney in Urban County, asked Mitch if he would interview a defendant for drug court. The assistant prosecuting attorney told Mitch that the defendant, Lee James, was being held in the county jail. His parents had called the prosecuting attorney, asking for help for their son. The parents said that their son had a serious drug problem. Mitch agreed to see the defendant.

On July 10, Lee came to Mitch's office for an interview. Before the interview, Mitch had learned from the case file that Lee was charged with numerous forgery charges in which it was alleged that he had stolen his parents' blank checks and had written bad checks. The charges were neither violent nor serious, Mitch believed. Given that Lee's parents were the victims and they had requested that their son enter drug court, Mitch knew that the necessary victim's approval for a drug court applicant to enter the program was assured.

During the interview, Lee told Mitch that he had a drug problem. Lee reported regularly using several drugs, including cocaine, crack cocaine and marijuana. He had previously received treatment from three respected residential treatment programs for those with drug addiction. Lee explained that he would do well after leaving the programs and then "fall back into" drug use. Mitch learned that Lee was a divorced father of two children with a good job history. Currently, Lee was account manager for a loan company. Mitch administered a widely used instrument, "Simple Screening Instrument," that confirmed that Lee had a drug problem. Lee's previous crimes were DUI, simple assault and simple possession of marijuana, all from the late 1980s. After the interview, Mitch believed that Lee was a good candidate for drug court. Mitch asked Lee to call Calvin, a drug counselor, for an assessment appointment.

Three weeks after the assessment, Calvin called Mitch, telling him that he believed Lee would do very well in the drug court program. Mitch and Calvin made plans to admit Lee to the program at the next drug court session.

On August 18, Lee appeared at drug court. Calvin reported to the judge in court that Lee had an extensive history of drug abuse beginning with the abuse of marijuana and alcohol at age 12, cocaine at 16, and recently crack cocaine. Calvin diagnosed Lee as having cocaine, cannabis and alcohol dependence and recommended that he be admitted to drug court. The judge agreed, and the next day Lee began the program by attending his first group counseling session.[1]

Drug courts attempt to reduce crime through coercing and assisting problem drug users to become abstinent. Some drug courts are required to accept all applicants referred to them by criminal court judges (Hoffman, 2002a). In other drug courts, like the three that we studied, drug court staffers, primarily program coordinators, decide who to accept and who to reject. Drug courts, like other service agencies, typically cannot handle all potential applicants. Like other service agencies, drug courts distinguish between those applicants who are worthy or appropriate for their services and those less worthy or inappropriate for their services (Higgins, 1985; Link & Milcarek, 1980; Loseke, 1995; Miller & Holstein, 1996; Miller & Shutt, 2001; Prottas, 1979; Roth, 1972; Scott, 1967). Drug court program coordinators and other drug court professionals judge the potential of drug-using offenders to be successful in drug court.

In this chapter, we examine how drug court program coordinators and other professionals decide to accept or reject applicants for drug court. First, we discuss four important considerations that drug court professionals evaluate in deciding who is worthy or unworthy for drug court. Next, we examine the importance of advocacy in judging potential. We end by discussing how drug court staffers decide to reject drug court applicants. Within the established requirements of the drug court program, with a concern for the effective use of program resources, and within the organizational and political concerns of drug court,

1. For the first two months of the program, Lee did well, attending meetings and testing negative for drug use. He relapsed for 2 weeks and then resumed his progress. The drug court staff was shocked to learn that Lee died from a heroin overdose two months after his relapse.

professional staffers use their experience and expertise to judge potential.

FOUR CONSIDERATIONS IN JUDGING POTENTIAL

Drug court coordinators, such as Mitch and the coordinator in Suburban County's drug court, and other drug court professionals judge applicants' potential for drug court on four grounds: need, motivation, risk and capability. As we discussed in the previous chapter, drug court coordinators gather a wide variety of information from and about the drug court applicants. They use only the information that they interpret as relevant to the four grounds for judging the applicants' potential to succeed in drug court in making their admission decision. If the staff judges the applicant as unworthy on any one of these four grounds, the staff may reject the applicant. Applicants who have a serious drug use problem need services. This may be the easiest consideration to judge. Motivation, the willingness of applicants to participate fully in the program, take the advice of the staff, and comply with the rules, may be the most difficult to judge when deciding the potential of the drug-using offenders to succeed in the program. Risk is the likelihood that the drug court applicants will commit new offenses as a client or behave in such a manner as to jeopardize the safety of staff or clients and discredit the program. Program graduates that return to drug use or commit new crimes discredit the program. Finally, are the drug court applicants capable of benefiting from the program? For example, the applicants may have mental health or medical problems such that they presently are not capable of succeeding in the program. The drug court applicant who has a serious drug problem, who is motivated to change, who poses little risk to the program, and is capable of participating successfully in the program is the worthy applicant. However, judging potential is always uncertain.

Drug court professionals were certain that one never knew which applicants would succeed in drug court.[2] This had become folk wis-

2. While staff believed that one could not predict who would succeed or fail, some research suggests this is not so. Drug offenders who use crack cocaine, who have committed their first crimes at an early age, who are unemployed, whose current charge involves directly confronting the victim such as purse snatching as opposed to forging a check, and/or who committed a nondrug crime before a drug possession crime were found to be highly likely to fail (J. Goldkamp, 1999; Miller & Shutt, 2001; Peters, Haas et al., 1999). Admission

dom among the staff in the three programs we studied as illustrated in the following exchange between a drug court judge and Mitch:

> *Judge:* You have an idea of what is going on. You know whether they possibly may make it, will make it, or won't make it. Of course, the ones I think won't make it are the ones that surprised me all of the time.
> *Mitch:* I tell everyone that one consistent thing I can say about drug court: if you had to bet on who's going to make it, you would lose money.
> *Judge:* Don't bet. I would rather play the blackjack tables; you have better odds.

Consider Tony and Brett. Tony's drug of choice was marijuana, he had a limited criminal record that included a previous simple possession of marijuana conviction, was a college graduate, and he had strong support from his fiancée to become abstinent. He seemed to be an ideal client. Mitch judged Tony to be a low-level addict, someone worthy of the drug court program, not a criminal who also happened to use drugs. The judge removed Tony within three months of his admission to the program. Tony had tested positive on every drug test; he tried to fake a test; and treatment staff reported that he had a bad attitude in group counseling. His fiancée left him, and he failed to get the job he wanted because he tested positive for drug use.

Brett, however, had used heroin for over ten years with an extensive criminal record, health problems and poor motivation. While Mitch had doubts about Brett's chances because of the apparent lack of motivation and long criminal history, he still wanted to give Brett a chance.

---

policies could exclude applicants with characteristics that are predictive of failure, such as using crack. However, in Urban County, to exclude crack users from drug court would be to exclude the vast majority of defendants with drug abuse problems, which the court was designed to serve. Conversely, programs could admit those who are at very low risk for failure (known as "creaming") and thereby produce high graduate rates. However, these low-risk offenders often do not need a program as intense as drug court. The potential cost savings (i.e., future rearrest, court processing and prison costs) would be reduced for a program filled with low-risk defendants despite the impressive retention rates. Ironically, those who would most benefit from the drug court program are often at high risk for failure. Finally, many potential predictors are extra-legal characteristics such as race, age and drug of choice. Admission decisions based on these characteristics would violate the "equal protection" clause of the Constitution. Even using what appear to be race- or gender-neutral criteria in admission decisions, such as admitting only majiuana users and excluding crack users, discriminates against black drug users because in our southeastern state those arrested for using crack are overwhelmingly black. The judges, lawyers, and coordinators likewise believed that as a legal program, drug court needed to treat similar people similarly and not discriminate based on extra-legal characteristics (Goldkamp & Weiland, 1993; Miller & Shutt, 2001; Peters, Hass, & Murrin, 1999).

The staff strongly believed all applicants must be seriously considered. Mitch judged Brett to be a long-term criminal who used heroin, an applicant unlikely to succeed in drug court. Yet, Brett not only graduated, but he continued to come to court for many months afterwards to stay in touch with court staff. The people who graduated and the people who failed drug court at times surprised staff.

Unless a compelling reason existed not to admit an applicant, Mitch and other drug court administrators, who were interested in helping drug-using offenders straighten out their lives, would admit drug court applicants to their programs. A lack of need, insufficient motivation, unacceptable risk and/or serious lack of capability became compelling reasons. Lack of slots for clients in the program may lead to a delay in admission.

Need

Did the offender have a drug problem or not? Did the offender need alcohol and/or drug treatment such as counseling? Without need, drug court applicants would not be accepted. Defense lawyers and others who referred offenders to drug court often told Mitch and other program coordinators about the offenders' drug use in the referral: "She's got a bad drug problem." "Apparently, Marty has a pretty bad crystal-meth problem." "Yeah, he seemed like a user." "Robert was a long-term crack addict. Started using crack in 1989."

The offenders' confession that they had a drug problem established their need. If made, the confessions occurred in the initial interview between the offenders and the program coordinators. However, if the offenders denied having a drug problem, they were almost always rejected by Mitch and the program coordinators he met. This was so even when criminal history, comments from the referral sources that the offender had a drug problem or other information pointed to a drug problem.

Mitch assumed three possible reasons underlay defendants' claims that they had no drug problem. All three reasons were problematic for being admitted to drug court. First, they, indeed, had no drug problem. Second, they had a problem but were not aware of it. Third, they denied a problem of which they were fully aware. Mitch judged those offenders who denied having a drug problem as inappropriate for drug court; they either had no need or were insufficiently motivated to succeed in the program.

Claims by referral sources and by the offenders that the offenders had a drug problem needed to ring true. Occasionally, defendants in jail might claim that they had a problem in order to be released through admission to drug court. One jailed offender told Mitch that no, he did not have a problem, but he could get one if it would help him get out of jail.

Program coordinators sought support for the claims of need. In the initial interview, Mitch and other program coordinators asked many questions about the offenders' claimed drug problem such as "How often did the offenders use? How much did they spend? And how did their families feel about their use?" Program coordinators believed that financial, relational, work, and health problems stemmed from drug problems. A skilled interviewer could easily obtain this information.[3]

Motivation

Needy applicants also needed to be judged as sufficiently motivated to stop their drug use in order to be admitted to drug court. Motivation predicts success in alcohol and drug treatment (Joe, Simpson, & Broome, 1998; Melnick, Deleon, Hawke, & Jainchill, 1997; Simpson & Joe, 1993). Motivation may be cognitive or emotive. It is commonly thought of as an internal state. For those in treatment, motivation has three components: problem recognition; desire for help, and treatment readiness (Hiller, Knight, Leukefeld, & Simpson, 2002). Problem recognition is the understanding by offenders that drug use is causing them difficulties. Desire for help is a significant interest by the offender in getting help. It is not a specific plan or knowledge of a specific desired outcome. Treatment readiness is a desire for a specific form of help from a specific provider.

Motivation, however, can also be external. Domestic ultimatums, legal threats, and health problems among other conditions may create external motivation for the offenders to go straight. Drug courts work within this realm of external motivation. The inducement of drug court is the removal of legal threats if the clients succeed. Drug courts

3. Mitch and other program coordinators never entertained the idea that applicants were such skilled liars that they were faking their responses during the application interview. The coordinators never entertained the idea they were being duped or manipulated by applicants.

exchange treatment compliance by the offenders for some legal reward such as dismissed charges or probation instead of prison.

Drug court professionals used three actions by offenders as signs of motivation: expressing the need for help, revelation of embarrassing information, and self-advocacy. In the following, Sherri, a coordinator in Suburban County's drug court with experience in a previous drug court, explained to Mitch what she looked for in that initial interview with the offender:

> When I interview folks, I send referral forms to the treatment counselors. I actually write on them what I think of their motivational level, where they're motivated towards a change in their lives by what they tell me. Some of them will sit in here and the only reason they are here is that they have legal issues. That is why they're here. Others will sit here and tell me "Oh my God, I hit rock bottom. I really need a program like this. I really think I can pull it off." Others are disoriented, and they really couldn't care less. That is where I get my determination of whether or not they even really want to be in the program to begin with. To be honest with you, I am really right on the money. When my counselors come back to me, I will see low or no motivation, and it will be just what I wrote on the top of the note. So, I can essentially fill that section of the form just by talking to him. We have so much paperwork now with different things; I can pull things from the paperwork to see what their attitudes are and what situations they have done.

Staffers judged offenders to be motivated when the offenders admitted to having a drug problem and expressed a desire to change, not just to get out of jail.[4]

When offenders revealed what would commonly be embarrassing information, drug court professionals judged that to be a sign of motivation to participate seriously in the program. In the following exchange between Mitch and a drug court applicant, the female offender revealed a history of prostitution, which Mitch took as a good sign:

> *Mitch:* Why do you want to be in the program?

4. While there were no observations to suggest this, we believe it likely that the interviewer signals the applicant on the appropriate responses to interview questions. Such signaling would be subtle and the applicant must pick up on the cues, but to the attentive, there are signals for appropriate response. As such, the admission interview is not a process of calling forth the truth, but is created out of the mutual interaction between the coordinator and the applicant (Holstein, 1993).

> *Applicant:* I want to be a real mom.
> *Mitch:* Have you been out on the street? (Mitch asked this knowing the applicant had never worked legitimately.)
> *Applicant:* Yes . . . but I really want help. Seems like everything around me is falling down.

While Mitch believed that he did not need to know of the applicant's history of prostitution, the applicant told him. Her honesty impressed Mitch. If the woman was honest with Mitch, then she might be honest in group counseling, which is helpful for recovery.

Was the woman honest? Could Mitch's reasoning be supported by evidence? Mitch does not know. However, he and other program coordinators took the revelation of what would commonly be embarrassing information that was relevant to drug court as a sign that the offender was honest and motivated to change.

Program administrators took drug-using offenders' self-advocacy to be the third indication of their motivation. When offenders made efforts beyond what was commonly done to get into the program, program coordinators judged such offenders to be motivated. Twice Mitch relented and allowed offenders into the program who initially appeared to be poor candidates. Both offenders had long criminal records, were currently using large amounts of drugs, and initially came across to Mitch as unmotivated. However, they came to his office regularly and called frequently, asking Mitch to let them into the drug court program. In both cases, Mitch told them that he would admit them into the drug court program after they completed Green Village, a local residential treatment program. The two offenders did complete Green Village, were admitted into the drug court program, graduated, and did well afterwards. Staff eventually judged repeated contacts from offenders as an indication of their motivation.

Risk

Risk was an important and complex consideration in judging the potential of offenders for drug court. Were the offenders drug addicts who happened to commit crimes but not of a violent nature or not with the intent to profit or were the offenders criminals who also used drugs? Would drug court clients commit new, serious offenses or behave in other ways that may undermine support for the program?

Mitch and other program coordinators could greatly reduce potential harm by accepting only those who were judged to pose little or no risk. First-time offenders with mild drug habits, well-paying jobs and supportive families posed little risk to the program. However, the least risky offenders did not need drug court. Other programs such as pretrial diversion existed for them. If offenders with long criminal and drug abuse histories became drug free, then the program had made an important difference. The offenders' lives had dramatically improved, staff had experienced satisfaction in making a difference, and the community had benefited through reduced costs and harm from reductions in future crime, arrests, court sessions and imprisonment.

Mitch applied what he called the "razor test" in deciding whether to admit an offender into the program. As he often mentioned to others when he explained what he was looking for or not looking for in a drug court client, "If this person failed out of the program and killed someone, would the program look bad?" Would the program have been expected by politically connected people in the community to know better than to accept such an offender?

Drug courts existed with the good will and support of legislators, criminal justice officials, and the public. The courts were relatively new in our southeastern state. Funding was always uncertain. Many professionals in the programs volunteered their time, especially the judges. The prosecuting attorney was an elected official. Bad publicity could damage each component of the political and economic foundation of drug court.

Drug court professionals used past history to judge risk. Offenders with previous violent offenses typically were not accepted. For example, Mitch did not accept offenders who had previous charges of possession of a gun. His reasoning was that possession of a gun indicated willingness to use a gun. Further, criminals, not addicts, used guns.

However, drug court programs varied in what constituted unacceptable violence. The drug court in Suburban County did not accept defendants accused of criminal domestic violence; Urban County's drug court did. The federal grant supporting Suburban County's drug court prohibited the admission of clients convicted of criminal domestic violence. The prosecuting attorney in Urban County decided that offenders convicted of housebreaking would not be admitted to drug court. They were too risky, according to the prosecuting attorney.

While the policy of the drug court in Urban County was not to accept any offender with a history of drug dealing, discretion was exercised as to what constituted unacceptable drug dealing. Offenders charged with drug dealing known as "sell one, get one free" were not excluded on that grounds. In such dealing, users support their habit by buying a small quantity of drugs, part of which they sell. Program coordinators judged such dealing to be significantly different from that motivated by profit where the offender is arrested with several small bags of cocaine packaged for sale.

Drug court professionals judged offenders with a long and diverse criminal history as much more criminal, and, therefore, more risky than offenders with recent and limited criminal histories. Mitch and other program coordinators viewed offenders who had a varied criminal history of a combination of crimes like thefts, writing fraudulent checks, drug charges, shoplifting, and other run-of-the-mill economic crimes as criminals making a living through crime, not as drug abusers or addicts earning money illicitly. Program coordinators evaluated offenders who began committing crimes years before they began to use drugs as higher-risk criminals, not lower-risk drug abusers.

Drug court professionals also assessed risk through their confidence in those making the referral of offenders to the program. Trusted referral sources could reduce risk by prescreening offenders. Public defense attorneys were the most common referral source in the three drug court programs we explored. Given the limited slots available for offenders in drug court and the large caseloads for which public defense attorneys were responsible, they referred only some of their clients. To the extent that they understood whom program coordinators would accept into the program and to the extent that coordinators had come to respect their judgment, public defense attorneys and other referral sources helped assess the risk of potential drug court clients.

Capability

Did the offenders have the skills and/or resources to successfully participate in the drug court program? Capability differed from motivation. Needy, motivated offenders who were not intolerably risky may not have been able to participate successfully in the program due to mental health problems, lack of transportation, inability to get off work, child care concerns, and the like. In Farming County, some offenders applied for drug court but worked second shift when group counseling occurred. They were not able to participate. Some offenders did not have reliable transportation. Drug court professionals judged whether offenders were sufficiently capable to take the chance of admitting them into drug court. Sherri, the coordinator in the drug court in Suburban County, explained to Mitch what she took as signs of potential inability to participate in drug court when interviewing applicants:

> Folks that come to see me, I don't want to single this out, but the best way to think about it when someone comes and they have no idea how they are going to get to and from. They have no transportation; they really don't care about finding any transportation. I certainly say you need to make arrangements ahead of time if you are going to do this program. It is very time-consuming; you have to be at certain places at certain times. You need to feel out the transportation issue. So, when they start hinting round that they do not have any transportation, they have nobody that can bring them back and forth, that brings up a red flag. The other red flag is when someone is sitting in front of me, especially happens a lot with females, not that we discriminate against anything, women with multiple children. They have a tendency to come in here and get scared about where they have to be at any given point in time. And they have to take care of their children.

Treatment staff was dismissive of offenders who claimed to not have transportation. Many counselors remarked that if offenders could find drugs, then they could get to treatment. The drug-using offenders would do whatever it took to get high. They needed to do whatever it took to get straight. Such comments became justification for ignoring the transportation needs of those who could not attend the program.

Mental health problems could become an inability to participate successfully in the program. The brochure for Urban County's drug court stated that the program would not admit offenders judged to be "too mentally ill."[5] Professional staff decided which offenders were "too mentally ill." Sherri, the program coordinator in Suburban Coun-

5. No statistics existed for the prevalence of mental illness among the drug courts we studied. There were several notable cases where co-occurring disorders were prominent. Lizzy suffered from a bipolar disorder and did well with medication. She quit all illicit drugs and regained custody of her children. Courtney had a personality disorder, which led to frequent relapse and little progress in a pure alcohol and drug treatment program. When she was switched to a specialized cognitive therapy program, she quit drugs and eventually graduated the program. Her grandmother described it as a "miracle." Such remarkable cases hide the lack of systematic data collection. Nationally, 42.7 percent of those with a

ty's drug court, explained:

> Mental health issues are one of the things that can be a red flag. It is not always a red flag. Someone comes into the program that has multiple mental health issues, in addition to their addiction, it can hinder us on the whole substance abuse. If they are not connected either with a private physician or the Suburban County Mental Health Center, that is going to hurt us in our counseling. They need to be connected to those resources, receiving medication if they need it. You'll find that they get scared if they're not already connected to mental health and have kind of backed off from mental health. They haven't been going. They're scared to do that. We make them make their mental health appointments. If they don't, a red flag goes up.

In the drug courts in Urban and Farming counties, Mitch and the other drug court professionals evaluated the use of medication by offenders and their ability to talk, listen and reflect. First, were the offenders on their prescribed medication? Drug court staff frequently obtained a release from the offenders in order to talk with the offenders' mental health worker. From the mental health worker, the drug court staff determined whether offenders' medication was stable. Second, did the medication have a high potential for being abused? If so, that was problematic. Mitch once was referred an offender who experienced agoraphobia, an abnormal fear of being in open spaces, with Xanex being one of the offender's recommended medications. Xanex has a high potential for abuse, and the abuse would be difficult to detect. Finally, how capable were the offenders in talking, listening and reflecting? Program coordinators developed an impression of the offenders' communication and cognitive skills in the initial interview. If the offenders answered appropriately and had no strange behaviors, then staff viewed them as capable. However, one offender applied to the program wearing an aluminum foil helmet. This was a bad sign. Mitch rejected him because he was not capable of participating in the treatment services.

Drug court administrators and other professionals judged the potential of offenders for participating successfully in the drug court program. While the professionals assumed that judgment was inherently

---

12-month addictive disorder also have a 12-month mental health disorder. Those in the criminal justice system have higher rates of co-occurring disorder. Sixteen percent of all detainees have a mental illness and of that group, 72 percent also have a substance abuse problem (CSAT Ditton, 1999; CSAT 2005).

uncertain, they evaluated the need, motivation, risk and capability of the offenders. The advocacy conducted on behalf of the offenders could improve the likelihood that the drug court professionals would judge the offenders as worthy of the program.

ADVOCACY

Advocacy can promote the admission of offenders into drug court programs, maintain clients' participation in the programs, and increase the likelihood that the clients will graduate from the programs. Family members, defense lawyers, prosecutors, offenders and others may advocate for the offenders. Their advocacy can be coordinated or not. For example, defense attorneys may discuss with offenders how to present themselves to program coordinators as worthy applicants. All cases have some advocacy unless the offender does not wish to enter the program. Eventually, the offenders must become advocates for themselves. Here, our interest is advocacy for admission.

Advocacy may consist of three forms: referring the offender to the drug court coordinator; an appealing story; and working to overcome admission problems. The simplest form of advocacy was making the effort to refer the offender to drug court and ensuring that the referral occurred. For example, when a defense lawyer came by to talk to Mitch about one of her clients, she told him that the client was perfect for drug court and sent a letter thanking Mitch for the meeting, and when the client called Mitch a few days later after receiving a call and letter from his attorney, Mitch judged the effort of the lawyer as an initial indication of the offender's worth.

An appealing story was the second form of advocacy. The appealing story may have spoken to the need, motivation, risk and capability of the offender for successful participation in drug court. The story need not have been lengthy. When lawyers or others made referrals to drug court, they told Mitch and other program coordinators about the offenders. The referral sources more knowledgeable about drug court were likely to make their pitch relevant to the considerations of importance in drug court. Consider the following appealing story made by an attorney whom Mitch had met several years earlier but did not know well:

> *Attorney:* I need to know how you do things over there. I think this kid will do well in drug court. He is 19. He has a real bad history. They charged him with Possession with Intent to Distribute (PWID). He had 7.5 grams but it was broken up into a lot of pieces. He should have really been charged with simple possession. He's not really a bad kid, he deserves a second chance.
> *Mitch:* He sounds fine for the program. Why don't you have him call me so we can talk?

Mitch viewed the lawyer's pitch as presenting the offender as worthy and not a risk, someone who deserved another chance, second chances being a staple of American society and justice.

Advocates may work to overcome potential problems in admitting offenders to drug court programs. A previous criminal charge or the appearance of unsatisfactory motivation may place the offenders' application to drug court in doubt. If attorneys or other advocates strongly support the offenders' admission into drug court, then they will work to resolve those problems as Bob Tucker (Freddy Solomon's lawyer) did as we explained in Chapter 2. In the following case, the public defender made extra effort to resolve a problem after Mitch had rejected her client from admission into the program:

> Martha Brown, a PD, called Mitch and wanted to resubmit a name. Mr. Smith had been rejected by Mitch because of a life sentence commitment in Louisiana. Martha Brown had checked into the conviction and found it belonged to another Mr. Smith. Her Mr. Smith is black, and the imprisoned Mr. Smith is white. She gave Mitch this information, although they had discussed it several weeks earlier.

Advocacy aimed to create a positive impression of the offender. While it did not guarantee admission, persuasive advocacy made it easier for program coordinators to agree to an admission request.

Advocates who were knowledgeable about drug court and respected by drug court professionals typically advocated more persuasively than those less knowledgeable or unknown or less respected by drug court professionals. Hence, defense attorneys may have been more persuasive advocates for offenders than family members, the latter typically knowing little about drug court and not known by the drug court professionals. Knowledgeable and respected advocates might say little other than they had a client who was suitable for drug court. Consider Brian, a former assistant prosecuting attorney who was supportive of drug court and made many referrals to it and whom Mitch liked. Brian stopped by to tell Mitch that he had a client, Louis, for drug court. Mitch told Brian to have the client call him to set an appointment. The trusted relationship between the former assistant prosecuting attorney and the program coordinator allowed for a minimalist advocacy.[6]

Advocates who were less knowledgeable about drug court or unknown to drug court professionals may have presented less relevant information when pitching for admission. Byron, an attorney whom Mitch did not know, called to see whether his client, Walter, might enter drug court. Byron told Mitch that he went to school with this guy and wanted to help him out. Walter was arrested for DUI, resisting arrest and Possession of Crack Cocaine. He had a drinking problem. Back in college, his nickname was Otis, like the guy in Mayberry (of the Andy Griffith television program). He was single and had many friends in Urban City. He lived and worked in Coastal City but went through Urban City on his way to visit his family. He came from a real good family; his father was a doctor. His client told him that he had the crack for a stripper he was planning to go out with when the police stopped him.

Much of this information was irrelevant: the client's nickname, the parent's occupation, and the quality of the client's family. The criminal history and the drinking problem were relevant. Mitch interpreted the comment about having the crack cocaine for the stripper as an attempt to indicate that the offender may use drugs, but not that particular drug. When Mitch met the offender, he learned that the offender regularly used crack cocaine. A poorly executed advocacy did not help an applicant, but it did not disqualify the applicant either.

REJECTIONS

When program coordinators and other professionals have discre-

---

6. Program coordinators, like all human service agents who receive referrals, work with referral sources and make sense of the referrals. They may try to educate referral sources into sending "good" referrals, make judgments of quality of referrals provided by varying referral sources, and try to judge why a referral source made any particular referral or makes referrals more generally. Program coordinators and human service agents respond to referrals within the personal and organizational relations that connect them with their referral sources (Emerson & Paley, 1992).

tion in accepting or rejecting applicants to drug court, they do not accept all applicants. In Urban County's drug court, more applicants were rejected than accepted. In order to learn more about those cases that were rejected; we reviewed all paperwork related to almost 500 case rejections in Urban County's drug court between 1996 and 2000. This paperwork did not cover offenders that Mitch only discussed with some third party or that he only met briefly. The various forms used by Mitch as the program coordinator allowed us to study the basis for rejections from a lack of need, inadequate motivation, too high a risk, a lack of capability, and several other reasons.

No form in the Urban County drug court program contained a rejection category due to lack of need. Yet, Mitch and other staff commented to each other that some offenders did not report a drug problem and did not need the program. Mitch believed that the discrepancy between the office forms and his experiences and observations occurred because he, as program coordinator, either did not complete a form for offenders who did not claim a drug problem or he discarded the form and kept no record of the contact. Need is such a fundamental consideration for admission to drug court that apparently paperwork would not even be completed if need was not established.

Insufficient motivation was documented when the applicant made no contact or refused to participate. Both "no contact" and "refused to participate" constituted 17 percent of the case rejections. When prosecutors passed a case to Mitch that they thought may be appropriate for drug court, Mitch sent these offenders a letter about drug court. Offenders who did not respond to the letter were rejected due to their lack of contact with Mitch. He assumed that the offenders had moved or were not interested.

Some offenders were rejected because they refused to follow through with the referral to the treatment assessment or pled guilty to the crime instead of going to drug court. We have some information about the specific reasons as to why offenders refused to participate. Some offenders told Mitch that the drug court program was too demanding. Still others told him that they did not have a drug problem and did not want the drug court program.

The largest percentage of rejections was due to unacceptable risk, approximately 45 percent. Violent criminal history, previous weapons charge, current charges, and prosecuting attorney discretion constituted risky rejections. Of those deemed too risky, 21 percent were due to prior convictions for armed robbery, strong-arm robbery, and to a lesser extent other violent crimes such as kidnapping and rape. The prosecuting attorney decided when the drug court program was established that no one convicted of burgling a house would be admitted.

Previous weapons charges comprised 8 percent of all rejections. Offenders convicted for possession of a gun were never admitted into the program. However, those who had been convicted of possessing other weapons, such as a knife, might be admitted. Mitch worked on the assumption that conviction for possession of a weapon that was a knife would lead to the offender being rejected unless the information clearly indicated to him that the knife was an incidental object. For example, offenders previously convicted for possessing a folding pocketknife on a key chain might be accepted; those convicted for possessing a steak knife hidden in a purse or a box cutter in a back pocket were rejected.

Nine percent of rejections were due to the current crime for which the offenders were charged. Where written notes were in the files, trafficking was the most prevalent current charge that led to rejection. The charge was taken to mean that the offender was a drug dealer, perhaps even a major drug dealer. Urban County drug court did not accept those charged with trafficking. On a few occasions, the prosecuting attorneys reduced the charge from trafficking to PWID because they believed that the evidence did not support the more serious charge. This allowed the offender to be admitted to drug court.

Urban County drug court received some referrals in which the current charge for the offenders included violent crimes such as strong-arm robbery or gun possession. These referrals were never accepted. Mitch assumed that the referral source was unknowledgeable about drug court policy.

Eight percent of rejections were classified as "prosecuting attorney discretion." Prosecuting attorneys, supervising attorneys, or Mitch vetoed a potential admission. Being arrested in a special police action such as a drug sweep or having new charges pending became grounds for rejecting offenders. Having an extensive criminal record, even if not particularly violent, could become grounds for rejecting offenders. However, no stated or unstated policy defined what constituted too many prior convictions. One offender with more than fifteen prior convictions and three prison stays was admitted into the program and graduated. The last the professional staff heard, he was leading his local twelve-step self-help group.

Like the lack of need, the lack of capability was not listed on forms recording the rejection of clients. However, written notes indicated that some offenders were rejected due to the severity of their mental illness and their inability to participate adequately in the program.

Program resources and policies became the grounds for some rejections. Six percent of rejections were due to the lack of funds to purchase treatment for offenders from the contracted treatment agency. As the funds were dwindling, Mitch did not prioritize who got in among several applicants who were "admittable"; once the money was expended no one entered the program. At least ten offenders were denied admission because their victims refused to give their permission for the offenders to enter the program. As coordinator, Mitch had told many others that victim refusal had occurred only once. The records showed that his recollection as coordinator on this point was unsupported.[7]

CONCLUSION

Where discretion was available, program coordinators and other staff members judged the potential of offenders for successfully completing drug court. Drug court professionals aimed to select the worthy offender and reject the unworthy offender. The worthy offender was a serious drug user who had the ability and motivation to benefit from the program and did not pose an unacceptable risk of harming the program. The unworthy offender was the unmotivated drug user, the risky criminal, and, sympathetically, the addict who needed services but was not presently capable of benefiting from the program.

In judging potential, the drug court staff assumed that they could never be certain who would and would not succeed. Trusted and knowledgeable referral sources increased the likelihood that the pro-

---

7. Staff form perceptions about the applicant and these perceptions are "true" until revised by additional information. Such perceptions may not be supported by the totality of observable phenomena; another observer might come to a different "truth." The admission process involves many professionals and each professional has her/his "truth" of the applicant. In meeting together, these perceptions become modified through persuasion and negotiation. On the surface, rejection then is based on the client characteristics, like criminal record, and policy, such as a prohibition against violent offenders. Such surface explanation belies the complexity of accounts, interpretation, judgment and persuasion.

fessional staff would judge offenders as worthy of drug court. Yet, the professional staff in the three drug courts that we studied were also interested in helping drug users who could benefit from the services that they provided rather than simply making themselves and their program look good by taking offenders who were first-time, nonserious offenders with little history of drug use. All staff members displayed a deep belief that people should be given a chance to succeed, even if staff doubted the likelihood of success for some offenders who were admitted.

The drug court professionals judged potential within the organizational and political concerns of their drug courts. Otherwise qualified offenders were rejected when funds were not available. An offender who had been convicted for armed robbery thirty years earlier but otherwise had few previous convictions was rejected because he posed too great a risk to the program. Should this offender commit a new, serious crime while in the program, politicians and others in the community may question the judgment of the prosecuting attorney and other professionals for admitting an offender with a violent past.

When drug court professionals judge offenders as worthy of being admitted and treatment slots are available, the professionals admit the offenders to drug court. Will the drug court clients succeed? Will they fail? The professionals are not certain. But through providing services to the drug court clients and judging their progress, the professionals attempt to enable drug court clients to go straight. We next turn our attention to the difficult work of judging progress.

Chapter 4

JUDGING PARTICIPATION

One summer Tuesday morning, Mitch arrived at the office of the Urban County's drug court treatment program, New Start, at 10:00 A.M. to meet with the treatment counselors before drug court would be held that evening. Mitch liked the group of counselors and enjoyed talking with them. Mitch was greeted warmly by all three counselors, some of whom he had known for several years. As always, Jane gave Mitch a written summary of all the clients' progress. When Mitch finished reading the summary, Calvin began to discuss the clients.

Calvin reported that Chantal's most recent tests had come back "funny for amphetamines" and he had sent the tests to the lab for confirmation. Calvin added that Chantal reported being a little depressed. The amphetamines would take care of that, Calvin added with a smile at the little joke. Mitch agreed with a broad grin. Mary, a counselor, next discussed Shawn. He had begun to complain about his lack of money and missing work to come to the evening treatment meetings. Mitch said, "That is a bad sign. Shawn begged me to get into group."

Calvin added "I don't know; we will see."

Mitch told Calvin about the rumor that Wayne was faking his urine tests. Another client had told Mitch over the phone that Wayne had offered to teach him how to fake the urine test. Calvin added to Mitch's report that Wayne was "missing in action."

"Wayne had so much criminal thinking," Mitch commented. "Instead of being honest, he did something really stupid and then blames us."

Calvin replied, "Yea, his inpatient program sent their treatment summary. They reported Wayne had a lot of the axis 2 stuff." Mitch understood axis 2 stuff was bad. Wayne had a personality disorder, probably an antisocial personality disorder; in other words, just another thug, Mitch knew.

The staffing progressed to more mundane matters such as clients who were doing well. These clients were most often discussed in passing. As 11:00 approached, Mitch readied himself to go back to the courthouse and get ready for court that night.

Once drug court judges admit applicants to the program, the drug-using offenders become clients. Professional staffers provide services to the clients and monitor their participation in the program with the aim that the clients will become drug and crime free, turning their lives around. The staff members judge the participation of the clients. Are the clients turning the potential to succeed in drug court that the staff saw in them into behaviors that show progress in the program? Are they worthy clients or are they becoming unworthy participants? Given that drug court staffers assume that they never know which clients will succeed and which will fail, their judgments of progress are tentative, subject to change. Initial judgments are not firm. However, over time, drug court staff typically develops patterns of judgments about clients. The patterns become characterizations or moral identities of the clients, which drug court staffers use to understand future behavior of the clients. The judgments are consequential for the clients' participation in drug court.

We first discuss the criteria by which drug court staff judged the participation of the clients, what we call dimensions of participation. In the second section, developing characterizations of clients, we examine the components of and the process by which drug court staff created durable, but not unalterable, moral identities for the clients. In the final section, we explore how staff sanctioned clients and the importance that characterizations had for sanctioning. Through sanctioning, staff supported the progress clients had made and punished the violations and unacceptable behaviors that clients had committed. Underneath all the plans for treatment progress was the coercive authority of the court to enforce compliance.

DIMENSIONS OF PARTICIPATION

The drug court staff judged clients' participation in drug court on five dimensions: attendance at counseling sessions and other required activities, drug testing, payment of fees, participation in self-help meetings, and treatment progress. The first four dimensions may appear to be easily judged. Was the client attending all counseling sessions and other required activities such as court sessions or community service? Did the client test positive or negative for drug use? Has the client paid program and other fees, such as restitution fees? Finally, was the client attending self-help meetings such as Alcoholics Anonymous or Narcotics Anonymous? However, drug court staff interpreted the clients' behavior on each of these dimensions, especially the clients' noncompliance and the reasons they gave for noncompliance. The fifth dimension, treatment progress, relied the greatest on the staff's interpretation. Were clients developing an emotional awareness and cognitive understanding of their drug use; were they developing and using the "tools" to keep them drug free; were they developing drug-free selves, not just becoming individuals who did not do drugs? For example, clients may have been attending group counseling, but if they were not talking in ways judged as candid by the counselors, their attendance was devalued and the counselors judged them not to be making progress.

During the clients' participation in drug court, the treatment counselors, not the program coordinators, interacted the most with the clients and created the most significant information about the clients. For example, during the first phase in the program, counselors may have seen clients six to nine hours per week. Program coordinators and lawyers may not have seen clients outside the courtroom. The counselors' treatment framework for judging clients became dominant. Therefore, legal and political issues, such as risk to the community, while still considered, became less significant in comparison to treatment performance, such as talking honestly in group counseling.

Through phone calls and meetings with the coordinators and other drug court professionals and, most importantly, through their treatment summary notes available to the coordinators, the counselors shared their information and interpretations with the drug court team.[1] In all three programs studied, the counselors wrote treatment notes reporting on clients' attendance in group and individual counseling, giving drug-testing results, and briefly commenting on clients' partici-

1. At no time do we use any treatment program's internal notes or documents. All treatment summary notes are notes that were circulated among staff as part of the court process. All treatment summary notes have been substantially changed to protect privacy.

pation in the program. While the format of the treatment notes varied among the three drug courts–for example, a full page form was used in Farming County's drug court compared to a brief paragraph in the other two courts–the notes became summaries of the clients' behavior used for court. Through calls, meetings and notes, counselors informed the drug court team of the clients' progress on the five dimensions of participation in drug court.

Many notes also included the counselors' recommendations of what should be done with the clients. Recommendations included punishments, such as time in jail, or promotions, such as movement to a higher, less intensive phase in the program. We turn our attention to the five dimensions of treatment participation, and discuss sanctioning later in the chapter.

Attendance

Drug court required clients to attend counseling sessions and all other mandatory activities such as community service and drug court sessions. All observed treatment programs had a "locked door" policy. If group counseling started at 6 P.M., the counselor locked the door at 6 P.M. Being tardy meant being absent. Being absent typically resulted in being punished.

Failure to attend a mandatory activity required a documented reason if the client wished to be excused. Claiming illness without documentation would not likely be an excused absence. Written documentation was best; next, confirmation from someone else such as a mother; least convincing was the client's word.

No matter what form the reason for the absence took, the staff judged its legitimacy. For example, one client in Farming County claimed in court that he missed a group counseling session because he had to go to the doctor and that the written statement from the doctor had blown out of the window of his truck as he drove to court. Leon, the counselor, and Mitch were very doubtful. Some in courtroom audience laughed. The client's father then stood and told the judge that what his son reported was true. Mitch was surprised, but the judge accepted the client's story because the father supported it.

Drug Testing

Counselors and coordinators drug tested clients. Testing was intended to be both a deterrent to drug use and an independent verification of whether clients had used drugs. Drug testing was used throughout the criminal justice system in the southeastern state in which the three drug courts we studied were located. Drug testing occurred frequently, at least once per week for drug court clients. The three drug courts administered drug tests in random ways so that clients could not easily guess when they would next be tested.[2] Tests in which drugs are present are positive or "dirty tests." "Clean tests" are negative.

When drugs are ingested, they break down into more fundamental elements referred to as metabolites. Positive tests indicate that some threshold of concentration of the metabolite was reached. The National Institute of Drug Abuse (NIDA, 2000) establishes thresholds as industry standards. Drug court counselors and coordinators may use various drug-testing technologies (Harris, 1995).

Broadly, two types of tests may be used, hand-held and lab tests. The basic structure of the many different forms of hand-held tests is a repository for the urine and a field where the urine interacts with chemical agents. A wicking agent absorbs and transfers the urine to the chemical field. The field is a chemically embedded paper in which the chemicals react to the decomposed drugs found in the urine. If no drugs are in the urine, then a line appears in the field. If drugs are present, then no line appears. Counselors and coordinators in all the courts studied often debated whether a line had appeared or not.

Consider the following four "lines." Would any line be so faded as to be judged not present?

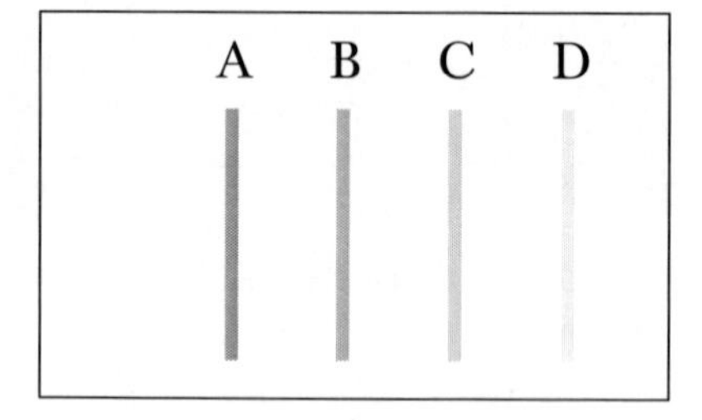

Figure 4.1 Sample Drug Test.

2. The variety of treatment programs involved in the three courts over the course of the study employed different "random" schemes. Some used a color-code system where clients call the treatment office daily. When the color assigned to them was announced on the phone message, the clients would go for a test. Other treatment programs would only test when clients arrived for treatment groups and thus the randomness of the test was only related to the random treatment day.

"A" is clearly a line, but with each step down the lightness of the color calls into question whether a line is showing. Some drug court staff interpreted what was recognized as a "light line" as "almost positive." The manufacturer of the drug test explicitly denied this interpretation, and no evidence to support the interpretation existed (www.dadebehring.com). Counselors at times interpreted the results of the hand-held tests in ways not supported by the science underlying the tests.

In lab tests, the urine is mixed with a series of reagents that determine whether drug metabolites are present and the degree to which the metabolites are present. The degree to which a drug is present is a "levels test." In levels tests, the number of nanograms per deciliter of urine is determined.

While lab tests were less subject to interpretation by drug court staff, some staff developed a "folk" interpretation. Counselors in all the courts studied commonly subjected clients to a series of levels tests to see whether the levels were decreasing or increasing. This involved biweekly testing. For example, if a client tested at 330 nanograms at test one and fifty nanograms at test three, counselors generally assumed that the client was not using drugs and was getting clean. However, if the amount of nanograms per deciliter increased, even if the test was not positive according to the standards set by the test manufacturer, counselors assumed that the client was using.

The science of the tests does not support the counselors' assumptions and interpretations. Many factors not related to drug use determine the amount of drug metabolite, such as the amount of liquid drunk by the subject (Cary, 2004). Drug court clients have cleaned highways for community service or spent a night in jail due to these "folk" interpretations.

Fees

All clients in the three drug courts studied were required to pay program fees. Program fees were $20 per week for all three courts for their first three years. After that, Farming County's drug court increased its fee to $30 per week. Clients who graduated paid between $1,000 and $1,500 depending on their length in the program and the drug court in which they participated. Mitch explained the fees as a "co-payment" made by the clients. He contracted with treatment providers for specific treatment services. The fees offset some of the cost of the programs, which was still quite expensive, between $2,000 and $3,000 per graduate.

The drug courts we studied operated according to two rules about fee payments. First, all drug court judges stated that no client would be removed from drug court for failure to pay fees. They may and did receive sanctions such as a payment plan for failure to keep current in fee payments. Staff regularly reported in court the clients' status in paying their fees. Second, clients were not required to fully pay their fees at the beginning of the program. Staff knew that some clients, especially those released from jail to participate in drug court, did not yet have a job or had not yet received a paycheck. Staff expected clients to pay their fees once they were able to do so.

Self-Help Meetings

Drug court staff expected clients to attend Alcoholics Anonymous (AA) and/or Narcotics Anonymous (NA) meetings at least twice weekly. To prove attendance, clients were required to obtain a signature from someone, often the chair, in the meeting on an attendance form used by the treatment agencies. This system of verification is common throughout the drug treatment community. However, such a system is vulnerable to forgeries. All staffs observed were sure that forgeries occurred, but the staff did not address this issue in court. To remove a client for forging an attendance form was rare.

Treatment Progress

Drug court staff required clients to attend counseling sessions. They expected them, however, to participate in the counseling through talk that counselors judged to be honest, self-revealing, and accepting of responsibility for drug use and for their behavior. Counselors' evaluations of the clients' participation in group counseling (and, for fewer clients, in individual counseling) became the clients' treatment progress. In the following paraphrased treatment note, a counselor has commented about a client's level and type of participation:

> Client is making progress with speaking the true and difficult things about himself. Progress is satisfactory.

The language the counselors used to report the clients' progress reflected their treatment orientation. Mitch and other program coordinators had the responsibility of explaining what the counselor meant in nontherapeutic terms to the judges and lawyers. For example, a counselor who worked in a treatment agency that used a therapeutic community approach wrote in a treatment note that a client "expressed that he has not surrendered, nor humbled himself to his addiction, doesn't like being sober and drug free." Mitch would explain to a judge or lawyer that the counselor meant the client did not agree with the staff and likely argued with them. Counselors working within the Minnesota Model commonly reported a client was "working a program of recovery." After a few explanations from the program coordinator, judges and lawyers readily understood what the counselors meant.

DEVELOPING CHARACTERIZATIONS OF CLIENTS

As drug court staff provided treatment and monitored clients' participation in the program, they eventually came to characterize clients as having varying moral identities. Characterizing clients developed over the months, even a year or more, that the clients participated in drug court. Staff used characterizations, the durable, but not unalterable, moral identities they attributed to clients, to explain clients' behavior. Without always being aware of doing so, staff used characterizations in sanctioning clients for behavior judged more or less acceptable.

First, we discuss clients' movements between phases in the treatment program. Phases were the official designation of clients' location within the treatment program from admission to graduation. Staff used phases in evaluating clients' behavior. Next, we take up "tools," the treatment staff metaphor for the understandings of and approaches for dealing with drug use that clients were expected to develop during treatment. Not having acquired the tools or not using the tools became staff explanations for clients who continued to use drugs. Third, staff interpreted some behaviors by clients as signs of their likely future behavior. Some signs were good; others, bad. Fourth, as staff worked with clients, they developed and used folk explanations to make sense of the clients' drug-court behavior, particularly their failures. The folk explanations provided what counselors took to be a more comprehensive understanding of the clients. Finally, through repeated interactions with clients and judgments of them, staff came to characterize the clients as more or less worthy drug court clients.

PHASES AND EXPECTATIONS

In the three drug courts we studied, treatment programs were composed of three or four phases. Differing requirements for the clients characterized each phase. Phase 1 was the most intensive; Phase 3 or 4, the least intensive. In Phase 1, clients were required to attend three group counseling sessions each week, two self-help meetings, and submit to a drug test at least once each week, though sometimes twice per week. In Phase 2, clients went to group counseling twice each week and were less likely to be drug tested twice in a given week. They continued to go to self-help meetings. Group counseling was reduced to once per week in Phase 3 and to twice per month in Phase 4.[3]

As clients progressed from one phase to the next, staff's expectations for the clients became more demanding. Staff held relatively low expectations when clients entered the program. They expected that clients would miss some meetings, test positive for drug use, and not necessarily talk honestly about themselves in group counseling. By Phase 4, staff expected that clients would walk into group counseling sessions and talk honestly and deeply about sobriety, drug use or other relevant topics and that they would consistently not be using drugs. Clients were gaining skills to avoid drug use in Phase 1; by Phase 4 they should be using their skills.

In the following interview excerpt, Calvin, a long-time counselor with the drug court programs in Urban and Suburban counties, discussed with Mitch a client, Vickie, who was removed from drug court in Urban County after participating almost one year. Calvin noted that expectations for clients shifted by what phase the clients were in:

> Being closed and fear of being put down. Those were things we dealt with in Phase 1. We tried to get her to participate. The behaviors of Phase 1 tend to reappear in Phase 3. That is the most difficult phase in the program. The only difference is they tend to have more clean time.

---

3. Recall from our earlier discussion the number of phases varied by treatment program. The majority of programs had three phases, while a couple of the programs divided the course into 4 phases.

> But the old behaviors tend to come back. That is something we tell people; we shouldn't have to coerce people, and we shouldn't have to tell the core people. At this time, we don't expect things to be perfect, but at least expect the later part of Phase 2 people and definitely Phase 3 people to walk through the door and be able to say, "I need help. I'm not on stable ground."[4]

Drug court staff promoted clients to higher phases and occasionally demoted clients to lower phases as they judged clients to have progressed in treatment. As staff promoted (or demoted) clients, they came to hold different expectations for the clients. Promotions (and demotions) reflected the staff's continuing assignment of moral worth to the clients, which had begun when the clients applied to drug court.

TOOLS

Treatment staff often used the term "tools" when speaking of the progress or lack of progress of drug court clients. Tools referred to the ways drug users could successfully handle their desire to use drugs when that desire was experienced. Tools could include going to a self-help meeting, calling a sponsor or talking to a family member. In the following conversation between Mitch and Katie, a counselor in the drug court in Suburban County, Katie described what it meant to use tools and gave some examples:

> *Katie:* They (i.e., clients) get more involved. They use their tools. You can just tell by what they are saying if they are using their tools. They do not know they are telling on themselves.
> *Mitch:* What do you mean by "using their tools"?
> *Katie:* Tools of recovery. Jonathan is one example.
> *Mitch:* Which one?
> *Katie:* He is upset with the staff changing. He has caught a meeting every day. He has talked to his sponsor. He has come in here without an individual appointment and talked with me for an hour and a half.

4. Phase movement harkens back to the idea of status passage. Glaser and Strauss examined how the temporal aspects of dying affected the treatment of the patient by the staff. Other authors have characterized religious conversion, slaves running away, divorcing women, high school graduates' first jobs, and near-death experiences as status passages. In all these examples, the authors use status passage to describe the movement of a given person from one place in a social structure to another (Glaser & Strauss, 1965). They called this idea "status passage" (Gallant, 1992; Harris, 1980; Hubner, 1983; Kellehear, 1990; Ward, 1980).

> On another day, he called me. He is trying to work through it without using. He has gotten to where now he has enough feeling about his addiction.
> *Mitch:* He is actively engaged with people in that he goes to meetings, he is talking to his sponsor, and he really wants to talk to you about what's going on and your leaving and how it makes him feel.

Staff members assumed that when clients first enter the program, they typically lacked the tools to deal successfully with their desire to use drugs. Whether the clients were sufficiently motivated to change when they entered the program, staff assumed that they did not know how to quit; they lacked the tools.

Staff commonly explained clients returning to drug use after the clients had been making important progress in treatment by claiming that the clients were not using their tools. Vickie, a client mentioned earlier, had done well for many months but then returned to using drugs. When staff discussed why she failed the program, a consensus quickly emerged that she did not apply her tools when she began to experience problems in her dating relationships. One of Vickie's counselors, Teddy, mentioned that Vickie did not use her tools:

> Vickie is at that point now, "Do you really want it or not?" You know she goes out there and doesn't use her tools. She didn't talk to anyone about her feelings that carried her through the phases. Perfect your use of those tools, not just carry them around. It is like going to the emergency room bleeding. You wait two hours and then go in the parking lot and die. That is what Vickie did.

The client metaphorically "bled to death" rather than using the tools she had acquired. Perhaps her motivation had waned. To the staff, her failure was her fault.

SIGNS

Drug court staff used client behavior as indications of where the clients were headed in the program. Some behaviors were good signs; others, bad. Signs could come at any time. They need not be dramatic. Signs developed out of the staff's professional experiences. Often the staff had seen previous clients display a behavior before they failed or a different set of behaviors when other clients succeeded.

Staff viewed compliance with drug court, clean drug tests, attentiveness, and self-disclosure in counseling as good signs for clients early in the program. Other good signs were helping fellow clients in the group such as offering rides to clients without rides or offering one's phone number to another client "if the client needed some help." Some drug court clients made plans with fellow clients to attend self-help meetings together. Attending group counseling sessions or extra self-help meetings could be good signs. Mitch interpreted one client's taking notes on educational information in group counseling to be a good sign.

In contrast to good signs were bad signs. Staff interpreted, at times, noncompliant behavior; failure to take responsibilities for one's noncompliant behavior, including excuses and lies; glorification of street life; failure to pay attention in counseling, telling counselors they were wrong and other behaviors taken to be indicative of a hostile attitude; attacking other clients in group counseling; and other client actions as bad signs. If clients did not change, they were headed for failure.

For example, Calvin, a counselor, was very upset that James was attacking the new client in group counseling and that he was "high as a kite." James refused to focus on himself. Calvin understood James' behavior as a sign that he would not deal with his own drug use, being too focused on others. James eventually failed the program.

Faking a drug test was an especially bad sign. A fake test casts a pall over the remainder of treatment, always a seed of doubt even when good signs were displayed. Mitch could not recall, nor did the fieldnotes reveal, a case where someone faked a test and graduated the program (Mackinem & Higgins, 2007).

Two common ways that clients faked their drug tests were using another person's urine sample and dipping. Dipping, the adding of water, often from the toilet, to the urine sample, was a primitive attempt to hide drug use and easily detected by staff. Dipped urine samples would be cold to the touch or register beneath body temperature. Mitch always reacted with anger when he caught a client dipping.

Bringing in a false sample required more forethought than dipping. The client had to secure and secrete a clean specimen of urine. Secreting a clean sample of urine could become quite elaborate. A squeeze bottle in the underwear or inserted in the vagina was a common tactic used by those who brought in a false sample.

Mitch learned of one client in Suburban County's drug court who bought over the Internet a complete rig with fake penis, tubing, and reservoir. The counselors caught the client when they asked him to give two urine samples, one taken within minutes of the first sample. The counselors had become suspicious because the client's "behaviors didn't match his samples." For example, if a client frequently misses group counseling sessions and then tests clean, the behavior does not match the testing results.

Good and bad signs were part of the interpretations that staff made of clients as clients participated in the drug court program. Staff understood good and bad signs as indications of where the clients were likely headed in the program if they did not significantly change their behavior. As the clients participated in the programs, perhaps heading toward failure or success in the staff's view, the staff developed folk explanations to make more comprehensive sense of the clients and their behaviors.

FOLK EXPLANATIONS

In staffings and in phone and other conversations, drug court professionals discussed clients' behavior. Based on personal experience and beliefs; professional training, orientation, and experiences; and drug court responsibilities, staff explained specific violations and other inappropriate behaviors of the clients. Within the larger context of the staff's recollection of clients' participation in drug court and their developing beliefs about the clients, staff used folk explanations to make sense of specific behavior by clients. Staff may agree or disagree in their folk explanations.

Folk explanations centered on the five dimensions of client participation, which were the core elements in staff reports and discussions. An important component of folk explanations was the interpretation of clients' responsibility for program violations and other unacceptable behavior. Some folk explanations minimized the clients' responsibility; other explanations emphasized it, and, thereby, heightened the seriousness of the clients' unsatisfactory conduct. How staff explained inappropriate behavior directly affected staff recommendations.[5]

---

5. Our fieldnotes cannot speak to whether folk explanations have a direct, observable effect on the sanctioning of clients.

Consider Mark, Kerry, and Sara, three clients who had tested positive for drug use. Through folk explanations, staff interpreted their drug use differently, placing them in different social and biographical contexts. Leon, the counselor, had known twenty-year-old Mark for over ten years. Leon offered a folk explanation of Mark's drug use when Mitch asked him about it:

> When reading Leon's treatment note about Mark, Mitch noticed that he tested positive for cocaine on October 25 and again on October 30. Mitch thought to himself that this probably represented two separate times of use since the number of days between the events was longer than the time cocaine stays in one's body. Mitch commented to Leon, "So he has switched to cocaine?"
>
> Leon replied that Mark is still having problems with girls. "The little girls are about to drive him crazy." This was a reference to a previous conversation where Leon had commented that Mark seemed to relapse around dating or partying with a variety of girls.

Through a folk explanation that emphasized "the little girls," Leon minimized Mark's culpability for his drug use. Later, the "girls" became one girl, Amy. According to local rumor, Amy was a drug dealer and a manipulative woman. Blaming Amy for Mark's drug use minimized his responsibility for many of his future positive tests. Mitch understood Leon's explanation to be that Amy used Mark's sexual desire for her to pressure him to get high with her. The counselor understood the client's sexual desire to be reasonable, and, therefore, the client's drug use was less willful and not as inappropriate as it otherwise would have been.

Kerry's drug use and Leon and Mitch's folk explanation about it contrasted significantly with Mark's case. Kerry was the same age and as sexually active as Mark. Leon and Mitch believed that Kerry's sexual behavior needed to be restricted for her sobriety. No one suggested that Mark not have sex. Leon and Mitch understood Kerry to have troubled relationships with men. She was having intimate relations with a man with a criminal record who was jailed within a few months of dating her and with a married law enforcement officer. The counselor and the coordinator explained Kerry's sexuality as a problem. Mark simply needed to leave Amy alone; he could have sex with others. Kerry needed to become celibate.

When staff explained the inappropriate behavior of clients as other than the clients' direct responsibility, they were most likely to point to the influence of another person on the clients' conduct. Consider Leon's explanation to Mitch about Sara's positive drug test:

> In the pre-court meeting, Leon told Mitch that Sara had tested positive for cocaine. Mitch asked what had happened. Leon told him that she had let her old boyfriend move in with her in order to help with the bills. The boyfriend still used, and she used with him. Leon derided the boyfriend's paying of bills, "What is left after he gets high all weekend, he might give her some of that. Ain't much!"
>
> Mitch remarked, "If he stays, she might as well go upstairs and plead guilty, because there is no way she will make it."
>
> Leon later added more information: the father was a drug user and was presently in prison. That, in part, further explained to Leon why Sara had such a problem.

Leon lessened Sara's responsibility for her drug use through reference to how she addressed her financial need and to her father's criminal and drug behavior. Sara continued in the program for about two more weeks after this pre-court meeting and then was not seen again. Through folk explanations, staff made sense of clients' inappropriate behavior, accounting for positive drug tests and other violations in ways that lessened or emphasized their responsibility (Scott & Lyman, 1970).

To finish what happened to Mark, several months after Mitch and Leon discussed Mark's cocaine use in October, Leon recommended that Mark graduate from the program. Leon claimed that Mark had completed all of his treatment goals. Mitch disagreed, arguing that less than a month earlier Mark had relapsed on heroin and that two weeks earlier he had been arrested for domestic violence. To Leon, both problems involved Amy and were, therefore, excusable. Amy got Mark to use drugs and she had him arrested for domestic violence. Eventually Mark graduated, but only after Amy had legal troubles of her own and Mark found a new sexual partner.

When responsibility is lessened for program violations, punishment may be lessened, too (Weiner, 1995). Positive sanctions may even be offered. Consider the case of Gray. Gray had been in the program almost five months when Mitch reported on him in court. He had failed to deliver a urine sample. Jane and the other treatment counselors described Gary as being active in group and doing some "good work."

Mitch reported, "Your honor I would like to call Gray Neil. Gray continues to do well in the program, but it is my understanding that Gray made the drug test but was unable to deliver a sample. We're going to recommend four hours of community service. I haven't done this in awhile, but since he has done so well if he will make an extra self-help meeting, we will waive the community service."

Attending a meeting is both therapeutic and social. It is shorter and less onerous than community service. Gray also received public praise, despite the rule violation. The treatment counselors had framed the failure to deliver a sample not as a dodge but as a harmless event.

CHARACTERIZING CLIENTS

Through repeated interactions with clients and interpretations of them, staff came to characterize the clients as more or less worthy participants in drug courts. The characterizations were durable, but not unalterable, moral identities of clients that staff used in understanding and responding to future behavior of clients. Through characterizations, staff understood clients as certain kinds of drug court participants, not merely that the clients engaged in this or that particular behavior. Staff expressed the characterizations through short labels, sometimes quite colorful, even profane.[6]

Characterizations reflected evaluations of the clients' motives, summaries of the clients' behavior, and portrayals of the clients' future likelihood of succeeding in drug court. The characterizations were based on the five dimensions of participation. Staff did not develop complex or colorful characterizations for most clients. Treatment staff characterized many clients as "active" and "moving to the next phase." When clients were participating satisfactorily, when nothing remark-

6. Characterizations are similar to what Vogler called typifications in his study of an inpatient treatment program for women suffering from eating disorders. Typifications were an unofficial basis to codify and manipulate patients. Using two criteria–compliance and potential for recovery–the staff generated unofficial typifications. First, the staffers labeled the patient as a good patient or bad patient. Good patients were noted by their compliances with staff directives. They fully utilized all the treatment opportunities and relied on the counselors. Second, the staff looked for readiness and motivation. This led to a set of typifications that included "good girls" (good patient/high potential), "bitches" (bad patient/high potential), "blobs" (good patient/low potential), and "slime balls" (bad patient/low potential) (Vogler, 1993).

able or unexpected was occurring in their cases, treatment staff often recorded "continue" in the recommendation line of their reports about the clients.

The following passage from a counselor's treatment notes was nearly identical to more than ten months' worth of notes: "(Client) submitted 2 of 2 U/A samples both negative. Recommendation: Continue plan." The characterization, "continue," gave the client the moral identity of someone who was worthy of the program's efforts, represented no threat to the program, and could at least be minimally trusted. Many clients participated satisfactorily and unremarkably. The staff's characterizations of them were simple.

Staff created richer characterizations for clients who participated inadequately in the program or who participated exceptionally well. In the following, we first take up the variation in how staff characterized drug clients. Second, we analyze and summarize the variety of staff's characterizations of the clients in terms of the staff's interpretations of the clients' motivation and possession and use of tools.

Variation in Characterizations

Staff characterized clients from highly positive to strongly negative, from the worthy addict who was making great strides in going straight to the unworthy, lying criminal who needed to be removed. In the following table, we list many of the common characterizations used by staff, what they meant, and the assumptions about likely future participation implied by the characterizations.

Table 4.1: Range of Characterizations

Characterization	**Description**
Criminal, Stone Cold Criminal	A very serious characterization and one of the worst possible designations given by staff. Someone who is not addicted but is antisocial and amoral. Troublesome to staff, many rule violations, shows no responsibility for own behavior. They have no knowl edge of how to lead a crime-free life. **Outcome: Bad**
Big Fat Liar (BFL)	A client that always has an excuse or story for any violation of the program requirements, does not take responsibility for own behavior. Many little violations. **Outcome: Bad**
Slippery, Slick, Slimy	Like a BFL, this client always has an excuse. Staff feels these clients are getting away with something. They may not have many violations. Staff watches very closely. **Outcome: Bad to uncertain**
Piece of Sh-t (POS)	Someone the staff totally discounts, no hope of progress. There are many violations. Client is not smart enough to lie well like the slick ones. **Outcome: Bad**
Dealer	Someone who is not a drug user but whose arrest is a result of dealing drugs. Not suitable for the program. Likely to graduate and be rearrested. **Outcome: Uncertain to good**
Leader	Someone who has been in the program awhile. No violations, good compliance, and helpful to others in the program. Helps others to become sober. A very positive characterization. **Outcome: Great**
Stepping Up	Someone who has been in the program for a moderate amount of time and has begun to make a real effort to be more active in group. Stepping up is a good sign for things to come. **Outcome: Good**
Active, Continue, Working Hard	A description of a good average client. Comes to group willing to talk, few or sparse violations, pleasant to others. **Outcome: Good**
Good start, Potential	A client who has entered the program; is active in group, appears open to staff suggestions, and has few violations. **Outcome: Uncertain to hopeful**
Treatment Smart	Someone who knows all the treatment language, lots of previous treatment, but does not seem to make the real effort to change. **Outcome: Uncertain to bad**
Playing the Game	A client who has no real violations, complies and talks in treatment, but staff doubt if there is any real change in the person. Staff watches very carefully. **Outcome: Uncertain to good**

Staff in the three courts studied used these and other characterizations. Some characterizations were more likely used in a particular court. Stone Cold Criminal and Big Fat Liar came from the drug court in Suburban County. Staff in all three courts used Playing the Game and Treatment Smart. Mitch used characterizations originated in one court in a different court with no particular difficulty in being understood.

MOTIVATION AND POSSESSION/USE OF TOOLS

We summarize the variation in staff's characterizations of clients by reference to the staff's interpretations of the clients' motivation and possession and use of tools. The specific tools will depend, in part, on the treatment orientation and protocol (Boren, Onken, & Carroll, 2000). These tools can range from "replacement thoughts" to calling a sponsor.

As we explained in the previous chapter, for drug offenders to be admitted to drug court, the staff must have judged them as sufficiently motivated to become drug free. Motivation may be external–the coercion of the court–or internal, the genuine desire to straighten out one's life. Typically, clients who had just entered the program needed some external motivation to help them begin to change, though some new clients were internally motivated. These internally motivated clients had usually stopped using drugs before entering the program, and the program became support for their efforts, not the starting point for their efforts. Staff often explained client failures as due to a lack of motivation.

The metaphor of tools, as we discussed earlier in this chapter, represented the staff's view of what clients may need to do to remain drug free when the desire to use drugs became strong. As clients participated in drug court programs, they should have gained tools. Tools may or may not have been used depending on the motivation of the clients, according to staff.

By dichotomizing clients as being motivated or unmotivated to change and as possessing the tools to resist the desire to use or not possessing the tools, we can summarize the variation in characterizations in terms of four categories of characterizations. The categories are our analytical summaries; the specific characterizations we put in the categories are from the drug court staffs.

Clients who have acquired the tools but are seen as not motivated to use the tools are "treatment smart" or "playing the game." "Slick" or "criminal" clients are judged as not motivated to change and as not having or wanting the tools. Clients who have the tools and are motivated to change may be characterized as "average," "stepping up" (i.e., making progress or moving to the next higher phase) or "leaders" (i.e., those helpful to other clients in the group). Newer clients who are judged to be motivated but have not yet acquired the tools would have "potential" or be "working hard."

Table 4.2: Characterizations by Tools and Motivation

	No Tools	**Has Tools**
Unmotivated	*Slick* *Criminal*	*Treatment Smart* *Playing the Game*
Motivated	*Potential* *Good Start* *Working Hard*	*Leader* *Stepping Up* *Average*

During a morning staff meeting with the counselors, Mitch and Hal, a counselor in Urban County's drug court, discussed a difficult client, characterized as slick. Three other counselors were present, but they participated in this exchange with gestures.

> *Mitch:* He is very slick.
> *Hal:* A slimy, slick, Teflon.
> *Mitch:* If he could just take responsibility, I would keep him in the program. But he always has a story, and it is never his fault.
> Everyone in the room was in agreement that the program was "throwing good money after bad."

Slick clients offered a lot of talk to explain their lack of adequate action. Staff did not trust them.

In contrast to the "slick" client was the client who had made a "good start." Clients who had recently begun the program, were trying to understand their drug use, and were complying with program regulations, had made a good start. The following note came from a treatment report concerning a new client, David:

> Client attended six of six sessions, 2 UA, both negative. Client has gotten off to a good start. Client is presently attending regularly, taking notes on educational information. Client attends the minimum support groups. Overall, client is complying with the program, does what is asked.

Staff also characterized David as "meek and humble." Clients who complied with program regulations might be described as having "surrendered" to the authority of the program and its staff. Humble clients followed the rules and shared intimate details with the counselors.

"Leaders" had the tools and the motivation. Not only did they "work" a "program of recovery" for themselves, but they also helped other clients. Staff rarely characterized clients with the compliment, "leader." Sherri, the program coordinator in Suburban County's drug court, explained to Mitch who were leaders and her expectation that experienced clients would become leaders:

> I think that, from my perspective, as the client goes through the program that they should be, they should become a leader, if they are doing what they are supposed to, they are helping themselves and they are sober. They need to essentially, and here is the term, step up to the plate, to be a leader. They need to be recognizing and helping those folks that are coming into this program to realize the severity of the program and teach them what they have learned as they have gone through the program. Be a leader so that someone in Phase 1 can go to the person and talk to them about some things. I think a person as they show potential, they should become a leader. They need to become a leader. And they need to become a leader, and we need to continue to expect more out of them as they work through the program. Because what is going to happen if we just let them glide or stay average throughout the entire program when they get out of this program, they're going to be an average or, the word I hate is, satisfactory. I want them to be above average. I want them to come out of this program with something that they didn't have before they came into this program.

Leaders differed dramatically from clients who were "playing the game." Clients characterized as playing the game sufficiently knew the tools to get by, but they did not make a serious change in their life. Their motivation to change was low and external. As long as the court did not punish them, they were satisfied. Staff might become frustrated by clients who played the game. At times staff wanted to catch such clients violating a regulation so that they could "slam" the clients. The staff played "cops and robbers" in trying to catch the clients playing games. To catch these clients, staff might drug test them more or not promote them to a higher phase so that they could monitor them more closely.

Staff might view a typical progression for clients who succeeded in the program in the following way: clients entered the program with external motivation and no tools. They agreed to drug court because of pressure from family and/or lawyers or from the threat of legal punishment. These clients were in Phase 1 and had potential. Over time, clients developed some internal motivation. They moved to Phase 2 and were continuing to work hard. As they developed their tools and used them habitually when the desire to use drugs arose and as their motivation became more internal, they moved to Phase 3. They were stepping up. Somewhere between Phase 2 and 3, staff expected to see a "real change" in the clients. Clients would become internally motivated and project an "air of confidence." Staff assumed that graduation was just a matter of time. As clients prepared to live without drug court, they moved to Phase 4. Those who were helping others had become leaders.

Throughout clients' participation in drug court, staff judged their progress. As they repeatedly interacted with clients, staff characterized them as more or less worthy clients in drug court. The characterizations were typically short, at times colorful labels that staff used in expressing the drug-court identities the clients possessed. Staff used characterizations to develop expectations about the clients' likely progress and to understand their later behavior. Staff used their understanding of clients, including the understandings expressed through the characterizations, in deciding what, if any, sanctions should be recommended to the judge.

The staff understood the characterizations as indications of who drug court clients actually "were," not merely as reflections of their interpretations and professional belief systems. If staff disagreed about how to characterize the clients, which at times they did–recall the disagreement between Mitch and Leon over Mark–that disagreement was understood as due to the differences in the staff's ability or in their opportunity to see who the clients "really" were. The disagreement was not understood as due to the belief that clients did not "have" identities but were given them through the judgments of the staff.

SANCTIONING

Staff sanctioned clients as they participated in drug court. They punished, praised, and promoted clients. When staff lost hope with clients, they recommended to the judge to remove the clients from drug court, a matter we discuss in the next chapter. While all three courts studied used punishment schedules for program violations, the schedules did not completely determine the punishments. The staff exercised discretion, which provided opportunities for their folk explanations and characterizations to affect sanctioning. Sanctioning was intended to promote client progress, of both the individual client and perhaps of the group of clients. Sanctioning, especially punishment, expressed the coercive authority of drug court.

First, we present the methods of sanctioning that drug court professionals used. Next, we discuss the sanctioning schedules and policies designed to make sanctioning routine. Third, we examine the three rationales staff used for supporting sanctioning. Fourth, we explore how staff used their characterizations in sanctioning clients. Fifth, we review how clients' behavior in court affected the sanctioning and characterization process. Finally, we discuss disagreements among staff for sanctioning clients and how those disagreements were managed.

Sanctioning Methods

Drug court judges, following or altering the recommendations of staff, used a wide variety of negative and positive sanctions in the courts we studied. Positive sanctions included praise, applause, reduction in treatment frequency (i.e., less frequent attendance at counseling sessions), fewer drug tests, and movement to a higher treatment phase. However, staff rarely referred to these positive responses as sanctions. They referred to punishments as sanctions, which included apologies, community service, increased drug testing, increased treatment frequency, mandatory residential treatment, changing jobs, avoiding specific places or contact with particular people, paying fees or fines, writing letters, and serving time in jail.

Community service was one of the most popular negative sanctions in our three courts. In the drug courts in Urban and Farming counties, community service consisted of picking up litter along the side of the road.[7] In Suburban County's drug court, clients assigned to community service often sorted clothes at a local thrift store. When clients were sanctioned with detention in jail, typically they spent a weekend so as not to interfere with their weekday work. At times, jail became the

7. The monitoring of community services took place in a variety of ways. Early in the history of Urban County's court, a nearby town had a community service program and Mitch sent the clients to that program. Several times the program coordinator established connections with local nonprofits who, in turn, monitored the community service. If the nonprofit did a poor job of monitoring the clients or had little for them to do, the site was dropped by the coordinator. Several nonprofits declined the community service program. The local jail offered picking up trash along local highways, as an alternative to incarceration. Clients had to pay $10 to participate in this community service.

holding facility for clients until they could be sent to Green Village, a residential treatment program for drug addiction.

A brief review of our field notes indicated that for every instance of punishment, seven instances of praise occurred. While drug courts can be viewed as a vehicle to coerce and punish drug-using offenders, they were also places of praise and encouragement (Nolan, 2001).

Consider the following announcement by Mitch that three clients would be promoted to the next treatment phase and the accompanying praise and applause:

> *Mitch:* Your honor, the following people will proceed to the next phase in treatment: Mr. Matthews, Mr. Levy, and Mr. Shields.
> With this, there is general applause in the audience.
> *Judge:* That is a significant achievement for all three of you. I congratulate you and am proud of you. And I looked forward to working with you in the next couple of weeks.

Mitch has commented and has heard others comment that "clients work real hard for the judge's praise." This comment did not signal the judge's reluctance to praise the drug court clients. It indicated the value of the judge's praise to the clients.

While judges had the official authority to sanction clients, audience members also sanctioned clients through their reactions to client behavior reported in court. Fellow clients and other audience members applauded clients who were reported to have done well and when the clients returned to their seat, praised, patted on the back or offered other positive actions to the clients.[8]

The audience also reacted derisively to clients who were perceived as trying to fool the court, often taking their cue from the judge or other court professionals. Consider the client who faked a funeral brochure to be used as a documented excuse for missing treatment sessions. The brochure was crudely drawn, with dates that had yet to occur. When the judge commented to the client, "If you are going to be that stupid, try to be a little smarter at it," the audience laughed loudly.

In the following, Hal, a treatment counselor, reported to the judge about a client who had tested positive for drug use. The judge's quip elicited laughter from the audience:

---

8. Given the familiarity of the clients with each other, such positive sanctioning may be experienced quite powerfully, although we have no such evidence one way or another.

> *Hal:* The client is 3 for 3, your honor. He is also positive for cocaine. We call him Teflon Ron because nothing sticks to him. He is just not getting it done.
> *Client:* I do good until someone messes with me.
> *Judge:* You're real good at talking; that's your problem. You are used to talking your way out of trouble. Let me make sure we understand one another. Most of what you say I do not believe. (Audience laughs.)

Hal insulted the client by calling him "Teflon Ron." The judge characterized the client as a good talker, someone who avoided responsibility by offering long stories. The audience was cued to laugh when the judge bluntly implied that the client was a liar.

The drug court staff's and judge's insults and quips and the audience's laughter were forms of shaming. The audience's shaming, as it came from the clients' peers, may have been more powerful than the shaming from the professionals.[9]

Sanctioning Routines

All three drug courts developed policies that provided specific punishments for particular violations. This made sanctioning more routine and more consistent from one client to another than it may have been otherwise.[10] However, the policies did not cover all sanctioning situations, and the staff and judges also exercised discretion at times in what typically were standard cases. While the level of punishment would increase as violations became more pronounced and more frequent, standard sanctioning policies were less available as clients participated longer in drug court and committed more violations. In these less routine cases, staff increasingly referred to their folk explanations and characterizations when sanctioning clients, which we take up later in the chapter.

---

9. Braithwaite makes an interesting point in regard to shaming. He argues that shaming, under limited conditions, can help a person reintegrate into the larger social community. Shaming, within an interdependent community, followed by overt actions of forgiveness and reacceptance, can limit the effect of being labeled deviant and promote reintegration of the individual into the community (Braithwaite, 1989).
10. A 1999 study of sanctioning in Urban County's drug court found that the type of infraction was not significantly related to the type of sanction. Participants may have received similar sanctions for different types of infractions or different sanctions for the same type of infraction. Sanctioning was consistent early in a client's career, but became inconsistent later. We suggest that with time and familiarity, the characterizations of the client became richer and the opportunity to justify varying sanctions increased. Where policy ended, characterizations held sway.

While all three drug courts developed sanctioning policies, the policies varied among the courts. In Urban County's drug court, for example, an initial positive drug test or missed appointment resulted in four hours of community service. In the drug court in Farming County, clients who initially tested dirty served twenty-four hours in jail. A missed appointment seldom resulted in any direct punishment in Farming County, though clients stayed longer in the program until they graduated. In Suburban County's drug court, the first dirty test resulted in four hours of community service if the clients admitted to using, eight hours if they did not. During the course of our study, Urban County's drug court adopted the policy of lighter punishment when clients confessed to their drug use or other program violations.

Sanctioning policies increased the standardization of punishment. This made the sanctioning less work for the staff. Carl, the program coordinator in Suburban County's drug court when we began our study, commented on the standardization of sanctioning:

> It is nice to be in a cut-and-dried program. Don't have to get into each and every reason. I believe the consistency of the program is why the judge needs so little time to rule on the case.

Pre-court meetings also enabled judges to more quickly decide on sanctions announced in court.

Sanctioning Rationales

Staff justified sanctioning, in particular, punishment, on three, interrelated grounds: external motivation, for the good of the individual client punished, and for the good of the group of clients who knew of the individual client's punishment. Drug Courts operate on the legal theory of therapeutic jurisprudence, as we discussed in Chapter 1. Through sanctioning, the courts may increase the external motivation of clients to comply until clients can sufficiently develop their internal motivation.

In the following passage, Judge Callahan explained in court about sanctioning to a drug court client. The judge compared sanctioning in drug court with more traditional court punishments:

> Sanctions are not for punishment. If I wanted, I could punish real good. It's as easy to order two years as two days. Sanctions are like Chinese water torture. They just don't go away. They let you know what you are

doing is wrong. A lot of times, some smart people don't agree. It is hard to get in this mode after putting people in prison all day. Sanctions are not for punishment. If that means you don't like it, so be it. Sanctions teach you some discipline, but it has got to come from you. You need to know we are going to stick to you, and you can't get us off your back until you do right.

Drug court judges and staff in the courts we observed viewed punitive sanctions as means for increasing motivation and promoting compliance, not for retribution for wrongdoing. By promoting therapeutic change, punitive sanctions addressed the public policy goal of lowering crime by reducing the number of drug addicts. These good intentions of punishment justified the sanctioning policies and the recommendations made by staff.

Ironically, drug courts punitively sanctioned only those clients for whom they still had hope that the clients would graduate. As we discuss in the next chapter, when staff lost hope, they chose to remove the clients from the program. Unworthy clients were ultimately removed from the program, not sanctioned within the program. Sanctions were intended to help the clients viewed by staff as still worthy of the efforts and resources of drug court become drug free.

Finally, staff justified punitively sanctioning individual clients as potentially good for the group of clients. This justification occurred more frequently in the beginning days of the Urban County and Farming County drug courts when staff spent more time discussing sanctioning recommendation before they developed formal and informal sanctioning policies. For example, one of the first female clients in the Farming County court faked a urine test immediately before court by diluting it with cold water. She dipped. When Mitch, the counselor and the judge discussed what to do, they all agreed to send her to jail, in part, because they were worried that other clients might try to fake their test if they were lenient with this client. Punishing a specific client for transgressions "sent a message" to the group of clients that program violations would not be tolerated.[11]

---

11. Some evidence exists that "sending a message" may work in drug court. Punishing an individual to deter that individual's future inappropriate behavior is specific deterrence; whereas punishing a specific person to caution others about what could happen to them should they act inappropriately is general deterrence. The deterrence of punishment is thought to increase as potential offenders' perceptions of the certainty of being caught increases, of the time between the punishment and the offense decreases, and of the severity of the punishment increases. Sending a message to the group of clients through punishing a particular client may be a strategy with a foundation. Some evidence indicates that drug court meets deterrence theory (Stafford & Warr, 1993).

Consequences of Characterizations

As drug court staff came to characterize clients over the course of the clients' participation in the program, the staff used and referred to their characterizations in recommending sanctions to the judges. Positive characterizations might lessen the sanctions; negative characterizations might increase them. For example, clients characterized in positive terms such as "working hard" or "making a good start" might still receive jail time for testing dirty, but the sanction might come with little ridicule or few, if any, harsh words. Encouragement, perhaps disappointment, but not derision, might accompany the jail time. When staff labeled clients as leaders, the staff extended greater trust, tested less frequently for drug use, monitored less closely, were more likely to believe the clients' explanations for some apparent infraction, and recommended less punishment. In contrast, when staff characterized clients as a BFL (Big Fat Liar), they were likely to suspect the clients more, increase drug testing, monitor more closely, expect greater verification of explanations for missed meetings, and recommend more punishment. Clients characterized as a BFL or a POS (piece of sh-t) might still graduate, but they were monitored and sanctioned differently than those characterized positively.

Consider the following remarks from the judge to a client who was being punished for testing positive for marijuana. Staff members had given good reports on the client during his first 114 days in the program and were supportive of him.

> Apparently, you got off to a pretty good start until now. All right Mr. Cramm, here is the deal. The purpose of sanctions is to help you focus on your problem. Do 8 hours community service, and I don't want to see any more positive tests. I am inclined to throw you in jail but these people think you will do better.

The judged referred to the previous reports from staff that the client was off to a good start. That characterization tempered the judge's inclination to sentence the client to jail.

Consider, too, Walter, a client in his mid-50s with an extensive criminal record who had served several prison terms. His current charge was possession of heroin. After entering the drug court program in Farming County, he never missed an appointment or meeting. He did not test positive for drug use until after eight months in the program when he tested positive for cocaine. The staff members were at a loss to understand the positive test, and Walter denied all use. In court, Walter claimed not to know how he tested positive for cocaine when the judge asked him about it. The judge sentenced Walter to twenty-four hours in jail, the lowest level of punishment the judge could have given the client for testing positive. The judge could have sentenced Walter to jail for more than twenty-four hours for denying using drugs and would normally have required a client who had tested dirty to attend treatment services and be drug tested more frequently. None of these common sanctions occurred.

No one watched Walter more closely or with suspicion. Others treated him respectfully. At the next court, staff acted as if Walter had never tested positive for cocaine. Because of how the staff characterized Walter, they minimized his positive drug test. Staff did not mention his positive test when they talked about him in meetings, when they discussed that he was getting ready to graduate, or in presenting his case in staffing discussions. When he graduated, the judge commented about Walter's "little slip."

In contrast to Walter was Eugene, also a client in Farming County's drug court, who ran cable for the telephone system. The police arrested him for possession of marijuana with intent to distribute (PWID marijuana). Eugene was not a model client. Nine times he tested positive while in the program. After about six months, rumors circulated that he and another client were faking their drug tests. Leon, the counselor, and Mitch agreed to do a double urine test on both clients in which two urine samples are taken within an hour. The reasoning was that if clients were faking, the clients would unlikely have brought sufficient urine to give two samples. The second sample would be the clients' urine. Eugene passed the double test.

After Eugene passed the double test, Leon tested him more often for drug use, watched him more closely, and made harsher comments about him in court. He began to comment in court that "Eugene has met all the program standards but still seems to be gliding by, not making a real effort." Eugene asked Mitch in court one night why Mr. Leon was "out to get him." No matter what he did in compliance with the program, Eugene believed that Mr. Leon would not recognize it. Leon's explanation was that Eugene "got away with one." Both Leon and the judge believed that Eugene was a faker. They would "see him again" after he graduated. Despite much evidence that Eugene was drug free, he was never characterized by the counselor or the judge as changed.

Eugene did graduate from drug court, having never tested positive after the rumors of faking his tests, seldom missing an appointment, and paying his bill. However, Leon never believed that Eugene was anything but a con. Based on that characterization, Leon monitored Eugene more closely and spoke more critically of him. Several months after Eugene graduated; several drug court participants reported seeing Eugene selling heroin and marijuana. Was he? It certainly fit Leon's characterization of Eugene.

As drug court staff interacted with clients over time, they created characterizations of those clients. They used those characterizations in making recommendations to the judge for sanctioning clients who had violated program regulations. These characterizations may have led to variation in how clients were sanctioned for the same current violation. What may be viewed as inconsistency in sanctioning as clients participated longer in drug court can also be understood as staff's guiding their sanctioning recommendations by their characterizations of the clients. The moral worth assigned to clients is important in drug court, as it is in all courts.

Clients in Court

Judges often gave clients in court the opportunity to respond to accusations that they had violated program regulations. This occurred especially regarding the continued use of drugs (Mackinem & Higgins, 2007). When staff in the drug courts in Urban County and Farming County accused clients of testing positive for drug use, the judge typically gave the clients an opportunity to explain themselves. Suburban County's drug court judge rarely did so.

As we explained in Chapter 2, the drug court staff's professional belief system about addiction, treatment and testing underlay their expectations that clients lied about drug use; made bad decisions that led to drug use; might likely relapse while in the program, which was normal; and after sufficient time in the program should no longer use drugs if they were motivated to do so. Staff fully trusted drug-testing results while also at times interpreting drug tests in ways not supported by the manufacturers' claims about the tests or by the science underlying the tests.

Drug court staff encouraged clients to tell the truth. Staff typically interpreted clients' denials as lies, their confessions as truths. When clients denied using drugs, they often provided explanations as to why the drug test was positive but they had not intentionally used illicit drugs. They faulted the test, suggesting that the specimen cup was dirty or the lab confused their specimen with another. They argued that the drug test picked up the residuals of previous use, not new use. They claimed that they were incidentally exposed to the drugs without the intent of ingesting them, such as riding in a car where others were smoking marijuana. Finally, some clients presented medical reasons for why they tested positive. For example, they claimed to have received medication at the dentist or taken medication for migraine headaches or menstrual cramps.

Staff routinely rejected these explanations, though occasionally they accepted medical explanations. Tests were not mistaken. Residuals of previous drug use would have left the client's body by the next drug test. Incidental contact implicated the clients; they were with people who did drugs. Dirty tests from emergency rooms visits were understood by staff as attempts by clients to "scam" drugs (Burns & Peyrot, 2003). However, staff more likely accepted clients who claimed their positive test was due to taking drugs for a preexisting condition or claimed some other plausible medical condition.

Consider Kelly who had been in the drug court program for more than six months and never tested positive for drugs. When it came time for her to provide a sample, she told the collector that she had taken "migraine medication" and offered to bring in the prescription bottle. Before court, the treatment staffer informed the court of Kelly's explanation.

> *Judge:* You let us know way ahead of time of your medical situation. Thanks for letting us know before the test.

The client did test positive for barbiturates, but the staff never treated this as a positive test.

Kelly claimed a previous medical condition to explain her positive test. Other clients claimed a unique medical event. Henry, the counselor, reported that Alice, a client, had a "highly suspicious" test that was positive for alcohol. Until confronted in court, Alice had no knowledge of the counselor's suspicions or that her test for alcohol was positive.

> *Alice:* Oh my God, I knew about the test. It smelled bad, real bad. I have

been drinking a lot of water. Been exercising; walks, runs and biking. My dad is diabetic. All my relatives are on the needle. I haven't done anything wrong. I made the trip this morning to pay the bill, but the teller machine did not work. I would not have done all that if I was going to dilute my test. About the rest, I don't know.
Judge: From now on, all tests will be observed.

Mitch recalled that under limited circumstances the excessive sugar in the urine, common to diabetes, could ferment in the bladder and thereby produce alcohol. If not for Mitch's recollection, the client would have been sent to jail.

Staff marginalized new clients who denied use as still too sick to tell the truth. These clients received standard punishments for drug use. Staff judged clients who continued to use drugs and lie about their use as criminal, not sick. They were not committed to change (Burns & Peyrot, 2003; Mackinem, 2003b). Instead, they were morally corrupt, deserving of contempt and punishment. "You know he is lying because his lips are moving," Mitch wrote in one staff note about such a client.

Staff viewed favorably clients who confessed that they had used drugs even when the clients' confession occurred after the staff's accusations, as was typically the case. When clients confessed, they frequently added explanations of the negative influence from peers, family stress or a tragic incident that mitigated their full responsibility. Clients who confessed emphasized at times that they had made changes since testing positive such as separating themselves from former friends who used drugs. Some apologized for their drug use. If accepted by staff, mitigating conditions, claims of changes made, and apologies reduced the clients' moral culpability and/or showed progress in their treatment. This might lead to less severe punishment.

Consider Denny. He tested positive for cocaine and had another test come in as diluted since the previous court session.

Judge: Tell me about the positive test.
Denny: I had a relapse. I don't want to lie to you. I relapsed with cocaine.
Judge: What hours do you work?
Denny: I work from 8:00 A.M. until dark, some Fridays and Saturdays. No Sundays.
After a short discussion the judge gives Denny 48 hours in jail, over a weekend.

> *Denny:* I'm sorry for my problems, trying to take care of my family. I want to apologize to the court, my classmates. I am sorry; I tried to do too much.

Denny was understood by staff to be honest and did not attempt to deny his drug use. He showed regret and a little insight about why he might have used.

When staff reported in court that clients had violated program regulations or participated inadequately, clients may have been given the opportunity to respond to the reports. Clients might offer alternative explanations about what happened or why it happened even when they accepted the accusations of wrongdoing. If staff accepted the clients' accounts, then they may have reduced their recommended sanctions and not reduced the moral worth assigned to the clients.

Sanctioning Disagreements

As competing characterizations emerged, staff disagreed on sanctioning recommendations. Disagreements among the professionals arose out of their differing folk explanations and characterizations and different assessments about what would work best for the clients.

Judges, lawyers, treatment staff and program coordinators valued disagreement. Disagreement reflected differing views of the clients and what should be done. Staff expected that occasionally they would disagree. The frequent disagreement did not undermine the staff's sense of being a team that understood each other and worked together. Instead, the disagreement reflected that committed staff members were using their professional expertise and experience to make good decisions.

When Mitch remarked in an interview with a judge in Farming County's drug court that he and Leon, the counselor, at times disagreed, the judge explained:

> That is good! If you agreed on everything, you would scare me to death. I don't want you to. I have never seen a counselor and a program director agree on everything. This to me is good to a certain point. Both of you have good ideas on what to do with people. If you and Leon agreed on everything, it would leave me by myself. All three of us have different ideas on certain things; this is good. The more ideas we have, the better we can make a decision from different perspectives. We all see people differently. Whether it is a drug dealer or user, you see them

> one way, and Leon sees them a different way from what I've seen of them. We can't slam-dunk everyone we see. If you and Leon agreed on everything, my job wouldn't be the same.

While at least some disagreement was valued, staff and judges still needed to make decisions about whether and how to sanction clients who violated program regulations. Staff used three approaches for handling disagreements among themselves: individual persuasion, negotiation, and letting the judge decide.

When drug court professionals felt strongly about how to handle a violation and other staff were less committed to their different views, professionals may have been able to persuade their colleagues to adopt their position. Most disagreements were handled through negotiation or by letting the judge decide.

Through negotiation, staff who disagreed made proposals and counterproposals as to how to handle a client until an agreement was reached. In all three courts, negotiations occurred between program coordinators and counselors when they staffed cases before drug court and among the coordinators and lawyers in the pre-court meetings with the judges. Drug court professionals routinely negotiated the number of hours of community service, the number of days in jail, whether the client went to jail immediately or over the weekend, and other sanctioning options. For example, when a client tested dirty for the second time, staff commonly would discuss the appropriate sanction, community service or jail. A program coordinator might suggest eight hours of community service, and a counselor would recommend twenty-four hours in jail. The coordinator would counter the jail recommendation with an increase in community service, possibly to sixteen hours, and argue that twenty-four hours is just one day, but sixteen hours of community service takes two days. Such negotiation frequently ended with the client performing community service instead of jail. Issues such as the client's previous behavior and work schedule could be discussed in this negotiation.

Presenting the disagreement to the judge, including the differences in how staff viewed the clients and the proposed recommendations, was a valued way to handle disagreements among staff. As Sherri, the coordinator of Suburban County's drug court, remarked during an interview to Mitch:

> Let me give you an example. The counselors are recommending that

> the person needs to go to jail and await a bed at Green Village. But I don't agree with that, because I think this person needs to be let out in the community for another week or so to see if they can turn things around, instead of using one of our last resorts to get a person back on track. So, in a situation like that, we present both options to the judge.

While the professional drug court staff valued disagreements about how to handle clients, they also developed several practices for managing their disagreements.

CONCLUSION

Once drug court professionals admitted drug-using offenders to drug court, the professionals provided treatment services, monitored the clients' participation in the program, and sanctioned the clients. They assessed how well clients were attending counseling sessions and other mandatory meetings, staying drug free as indicated through drug tests, paying fees, going to self-help meetings, and making treatment progress. As the staff interacted with clients during the program, they came to characterize clients, to give them moral identities as more or less worthy drug court clients. Staff explained the clients' behavior in terms of the identities they had given the clients. For example, staff might explain that a client faked a drug test because he was a POS or a criminal. Staff sanctioned clients' behavior, supporting progress and punishing violations. While much of sanctioning was routine, as staff came to characterize clients and the clients participated longer in the program, staff used their characterizations in recommending to judges how clients should be sanctioned.

When staff admitted drug-using offenders to drug court, they made the decision that the offenders had sufficient potential to succeed in the program. The staff gave them the provisional, tentative identity of worthy drug users, worthy of participation in drug court. As staff treated, monitored and sanctioned clients, they developed more durable moral identities for the clients as reflected in how they characterized the clients. Staff increasingly interpreted clients' progress or lack of progress in terms of their drug-court identities. Were clients progressing sufficiently to graduate from the program or were they participating so unsatisfactorily that they would be removed from the program? Staff judged the clients' performance in order to determine how clients would leave drug court. In the next chapter, we begin this final phase of drug court.

Chapter 5

JUDGING PERFORMANCE

Tuesday morning at the staff meeting before court was to be held that evening, Mitch started the discussion about Darren by announcing, "I want him out." No one objected. Mitch thought that Darren had not been doing satisfactorily before his arrest Saturday night for receiving stolen goods. Given the new crime, Mitch saw little option. At the previous court session, the judge had ordered Darren to do twenty-four hours in jail for testing positive for cocaine. Now Darren had been arrested on new charges that were not drug crimes.

Mitch had talked to Darren at the jail Monday afternoon. At that meeting, Darren gave Mitch a speech about wanting to stay in the program and that he could do well if he had a little "clean time" (i.e., time free from drugs). Since being in the program, Darren had tested positive six out of eight times for cocaine. Treatment counselors reported that Darren had a "bad attitude and often yelled at staff and group members." Mitch asked Darren why he should let him remain in the program.

Darren replied, "You need to get me to Green Village, I need some help. I got to get off Regal Street (a notorious drug area). They (i.e., drug dealers) call my house and come by. You can test me. It won't happen again. I don't have enough clean time. I envy the other people in group. Got to get off Regal Street. I got to get some money and get out. My sister is Loraine Smith and she is a parole examiner. She said she would help me this time."

As Darren talked, Mitch noticed that he did not make an admission of having made mistakes. Instead, the client talked about what drug court officials needed to do for him and about his neighborhood. The client's talk blamed others for his decisions. Mitch also remembered the reports from others that Darren had a bad attitude. Mitch was unmoved, but promised to tell the Judge what Darren had said.

Mitch and the treatment staff discussed these issues and later did so with the judge in the pre-court meeting. Barring any new information from Darren at the court session, all was arranged for the judge to quickly remove him from the program.

In court that evening, Mitch called Darren, who had his hands cuffed before him and was dressed in black striped prison garb with fluorescent plastic sandals. Darren ambled forward from the jury box toward the microphone placed before the judge's bench. As he approached the microphone, two officers subtly moved around him.

Behind a large table, Mitch stood and made the report that Darren had been charged with a new crime. "Your Honor, Darren was arrested this weekend for receiving stolen goods. Additionally, he failed to follow your order to go jail on Friday, and he failed to attend his Vocational Rehabilitation appointment. Also, your Honor, he has generally received bad reports from the treatment program. They report he has a bad attitude." As Mitch reported on Darren's frequent positive tests, he concluded, "I recommended he be removed from the program."

Judge Brown looked at Darren and asked him, "Well, what about it?" Darren began a rambling speech about the same issues that he had mentioned to Mitch in jail yesterday.

Interrupting Darren, Judge Brown commented, "I had hoped things would go well for you, but I am afraid I am following the recommendation of these people. I trust what they tell me, and I rely on them heavily. I am ordering that you be removed from the program."

The deputies marched Darren back to the jury box, where the other two men from jail were sitting. As court proceeded, Mitch saw all three men move out the back door of the court. Mitch never saw or heard of Darren again.

As drug court professionals provide services to drug court clients, monitor the clients' participation in the program and judge their progress, the professionals eventually come to decide how the clients will leave the program. Will the clients be removed from the program, having failed to progress satisfactorily, and, therefore, deserving the harsh punishment that may come to the unworthy criminal from criminal court? Or, will the clients graduate from the program, having satisfactorily met the requirements, and, therefore, deserving both the recognition for having turned around their lives and the legal benefits such as dismissal of charges or probation termination. Have the clients become worthy or unworthy of graduation? Drug court professionals judge the clients' performances.

First, we discuss how drug court professionals remove clients from drug court, "kicking them out" as the professionals say. Kicking clients out of the program most often represents a loss of hope by the professional staff that the clients are worthy addicts who will successfully complete the program. Less often, removal from the program is the product of a sudden or dramatic action. For example, when a client is arrested on new charges, the staff's decision for the client's removal may come quickly, as in the case of Darren. We first discuss the sudden departure of clients and then examine the process of losing hope. Second, we discuss how drug court professionals decide that clients are ready to graduate from the program and explore the joyous ceremony that graduation can be. While graduation is the goal of the program, most drug court clients are dismissed. Failure is not unexpected; success is the hope.

KICKING CLIENTS OUT

Drug court staff removed clients through two processes: critical incidents and losing hope. Occasionally, a critical, dramatic incident occurred such that staff quickly decided to remove clients from the program. More commonly, staff removed clients when they lost hope, coming to believe that the clients were either incapable or unwilling to make changes. Losing hope commonly occurred at the end of a long series of clients' behaviors evaluated by staff as failures.

Critical Incidents

Drug court professionals occasionally recommended the removal of clients because of some critical violation by clients of the program's regulations or expectations. As a general policy, arrests for new charges carried the presumption of removal. However, under certain conditions, the staff waived this presumption. If the arrest centered on a charge that occurred before admission to drug court but was just now coming forward, then continuation in drug court was possible. Staff could overlook a minor drug crime such as DUI or simple possession of marijuana if the client was prompt and candid in telling staff about it. Teddy, a client, was arrested for shoplifting. He was drunk in a convenience store and was drinking a beer from an icebox, without paying for it. Teddy stayed in the program. Conversely, staff universally acknowledged charges of violence, weapons and drug dealing as reasons for removal. These would have been grounds for denying admission; they certainly were grounds for removal.

Consider Deshawn, a client who had only been in the program for three months. When robbing a bank, he wrote a note demanding money on his deposit slip. The cashier gave the client the money and called the police after he left. The police arrested him within moments because his home address was on his slip. The client had also left his checkbook and driver's license on the bank counter when he fled. While Mitch understood this robbery to be a stupid crime, probably driven by the client's need for drugs, it meant his immediate removal from the program.

Threats of violence or sexual advances against staff or other clients could lead to immediate removal. For example, after about five months in the program, a client who was gay, HIV positive and suffered from bipolar disorder began making a series of sexual advances toward other male members in the group.[1] The judge quickly agreed with staff that he should be removed from the program. Even had the client not been HIV positive, his sexual advances would very likely have been grounds for removing him or anyone from the program.

Losing Hope

Drug court professionals typically became concerned about the progress of clients who tested dirty, missed counseling sessions, and violated in other ways the regulations of the program. They increasingly gave such clients unworthy identities, as discussed in the previous chapter. The professionals began to lose hope. As they lost hope, the staff members gave opportunities to the clients to show that they could progress satisfactorily toward graduation, that the staff should not lose hope and abandon the clients. Once staff had lost hope, they

1. Bipolar disorder is an illness in which the person experiences extreme swings in mood from profound depression to euphoric periods of manic energy. The manic stage is occasional characterized by impulsive spending, grandiose plans, and frequent sexual activity, including promiscuity.

recommended the client's removal to the drug court judge.

First, we explain the staff's experience of losing hope. In so doing, we discuss two program considerations, program capacity and the good of the group, that provided organizational context within which staff experienced losing hope. After we discuss how staff experienced losing hope, we examine the process by which staff sought to remove clients from drug court. Four components constitute the removal process: advocacy, trials, record review and presenting the case for removal.

Experience of Losing Hope

When staff became increasingly concerned about the unsatisfactory participation of drug court clients in the drug court program, about their failures to comply with the regulations of the program, about their inadequate progress, they may have begun to lose hope. Losing hope was founded on the characterizations that staff made of clients over time as the clients participated in drug court. Earlier characterizations provided the interpretative lens through which staff understood the future behavior of clients. As staff increasingly lost hope, they portrayed clients through previous characterizations and through recalled behaviors of the clients. The staff interpreted the recalled events such that they formed a coherent portrayal of the clients as unworthy criminals, no longer deserving of drug court.[2]

Drug court professionals in the three courts we studied understood the decision to remove clients from drug court in the following way: Have the staff done everything possible within the program to help clients who are not performing satisfactorily? Was there any reason to continue what was increasingly seen as fruitless efforts to help the clients? Did the actions of the clients show that they were unworthy of the program's continued assistance? As the staff came to decide that "yes" was the answer to the first and last question and that "no" was the answer to the second question, they increasingly lost hope. Eventually they may have lost all hope.

In the following interview excerpt, Sherri, the program coordinator

---

2. Occasionally, staff gave a "Most Improved Award" to those clients who, staff believed, had made a "180 degree turnaround." This award suggests that clients can move out of a hopeless characterization. The number of such cases is too few to make any reasonable assumptions. In all three courts the most improved award was dropped because staff came to believe it was a curse. All those who received the award were ultimately judged as failing.

in Suburban County's drug court, and Mitch discussed removing clients from drug court:

> *Sherri:* My thing is, and one of the things we focus on: Have we run the gamut on this person? Have we exhausted every single option, from placing them out of their house into a halfway house or connect them to mental health or all those things? Have we done everything we possibly can for this person and they're not responding? We have given them a good bit of the tools in order to do all these things and they continue not to heed the message.
> *Mitch:* I described this to someone as when we lose hope. When there's no hope left that we can help them.
> *Sherri:* I agree in that respect, I really do. You just throw your hands up, and there's nothing more you can do.

As staff came to believe that clients had developed the tools to stay drug-free and had the support do so, but they continued to fail, the staff began to lose hope. As treatment and punishment did not work, hope was lost.

Consensus occurred at times with little discussion. More often, staff arrived at a collective loss of hope and consensus on removal through serious discussion. In the three drug courts we studied, staff typically used policy to support the removal of a client from the program, but policy did not dictate. Staff decided to remove clients as they voiced individually and collectively their growing loss of hope.

Consider Ralph, who was removed after four months in the program. Ralph was kicked out of a halfway house, which led to Mitch and other staff discussing his removal from the program. However, being kicked out of the halfway house by the house director was not a critical violation. It was part of Ralph's pattern of inadequate performance. In the following staffing passage, Jane, a treatment counselor, and Mitch discussed the removal of Ralph:

> Jane told Mitch that Ralph was being kicked out of the halfway house for not paying the bill. This concerned Mitch. Jane continued, telling Mitch that Ralph had misused the living assistance checks for his residence. Ralph had a lady friend represent herself as his wife and cash the checks. The money then went to places unknown, and the housing bill went unpaid. Mitch found himself becoming angry over this. He commented to Jane that he was going to kick this guy out and send him back to jail. Jane commented that he was doing nothing in treatment. Mitch told her that he could handle the addiction, but this blatant manipula-

tion for crime just really bothered him and he didn't have any patience for Ralph on that. Jane agreed.

Jane viewed Ralph as an unmotivated client who was not progressing satisfactorily in treatment. The halfway house manager called him "poison." To Mitch, Ralph was a criminal; his misuse of the living assistance check was not an addiction-based crime. Both characterizations were consistent with the organizational positions of the treatment counselor and the program coordinator. Both viewed Ralph as unworthy.

Later, Mitch talked with the treatment staff about Ralph in the morning meeting before court that evening. When Calvin, a counselor, summed up the concerns about Ralph, he did not mention the stolen living assistance checks but expressed concern about Ralph's persistent inappropriate behavior:

> First, he disappeared. He wasn't coming enough for us to touch base with him. We could never schedule an individual session to discuss his options with him. It was pretty much the same old behavior. He would come in high and be apologetic for one week. After that, he would be gone again. It was at the point that we couldn't get him to come in. We tell people, "If you screw up, keep coming back. If you keep coming back, there is a possibility we can help you. But you got to be here. We can't help you if you are not here." It was like the lies. The lies, the exceptions, "I swear to God it wasn't me."

To the staff, Ralph's stealing the living assistance check with the help of his lady friend was just another behavior of Ralph's that showed a lack of good faith in a growing pattern of inadequate performance.

Staff admitted offenders into drug court when they decided that the offenders were worthy of the program, that reasonable hope existed for the offenders to be helped in the program and to become drug-free and go straight. Staff decided to remove clients from the program when they had lost hope that the clients would succeed. The staff had come typically to understand the clients as willfully noncompliant, though occasionally the staff lost hope when they came to understand clients as now incapable of being presently helped.

Program Considerations

Loss of hope for individual clients occurred at times within two program considerations: program capacity and "good of the group." When the drug court program was full and potential clients were placed on a waiting list, Mitch felt significant pressure, usually from a sense of duty, to push clients through the program, including pushing clients out who were not performing adequately. When discussing problematic clients with counselors, Mitch asked whether the clients were ever going to graduate. If the counselors felt that progress was being made, however slowly, Mitch did not push for removal. However, if Mitch received little indication that the problematic clients were moving toward graduation, then he began to promote the possibility of removal. If the problematic clients were not going to make it, then Mitch had "10 who would."

When all three programs had potential clients waiting to get into the program, then Mitch and the other coordinators more critically judged the performance of marginally performing clients. In the following case, the client, Akeem, was recommended for removal after testing positive six times. More importantly, Akeem denied using drugs every time and once blamed the staff, "for putting something in my cup." Note that one of the reasons in Mitch's thinking for removing Akeem was program capacity.

> In thinking about Akeem's participation in drug court, Mitch was convinced that Akeem was more focused on avoiding responsibility than self-change. After the last positive test, he contacted the Veteran's Affairs to see if that federal agency could give him "better" treatment. Akeem denied using drugs and denied that anyone had told him about his positive test, although the counselor reported she told him in person. Given Akeem's lack of admission and the number of people waiting to get into the program, Mitch decided he should be removed.

When there is no waiting list and especially when slots were not filled, Mitch evaluated the marginally performing clients more generously and with more patience. Coordinators and staff used and referred to the number of clients being served relative to the program's capacity in deciding and explaining their decisions to remove or retain clients.

At times, program coordinators and staff considered the effect of individual clients on the functioning of the group of clients who attended counseling together. Coordinators and staff reasoned that removing some unworthy clients also served to help the other clients either by removing an impediment to successful group functioning or by sending a message to other clients of what was expected of them. In short, some specific clients were removed for the "good of the group." Not to remove an unworthy client might send the wrong message to other clients. Drug court professionals did not remove problematic clients solely for the sake of the group, but the professionals did consider how removal (or failure to remove) could affect the group or how afterwards it did improve the group. The concern for the group perhaps lowered the threshold for deciding when to remove problematically performing clients.

In the following interview passage, Carl, the program coordinator of the drug court in Suburban County, and Mitch were discussing some recent clients removed from Carl's program. Notice Carl's claim that removing several clients helped the functioning of the group, but also notice how Carl characterized those he removed.

> Carl told Mitch that a couple of weeks ago he kicked four people out of the program. Since then, the program has been "rocking." Carl described these people as "full of sh-t."

Staff occasionally argued that removing a bad client was necessary in order to send the appropriate message to the clients that drug court was to be taken seriously.

Removal Process

As staff began to lose hope, they increasingly considered removing the client. However, advocates for a client, particularly professional staff who had not lost hope, could forestall the move toward removal. Second, if staff moved toward removal, at least in the three courts we studied, staff provided final opportunities for the clients to perform adequately, to show the staff that they should not lose hope, and that the clients were worthy of further assistance in drug court. We call these opportunities "trials." Finally, if the clients had not passed the trials, then the program coordinator thoroughly reviewed the clients' case records in order to identify the grounds that would be presented to the judge for the clients' removal. Infrequently, the record review led the professional staff not to recommend removal of clients, at least at that time.

Advocacy

When some staff members lost hope and began to urge that unworthy clients be removed from drug court, other staff members may not have lost hope. These hopeful staff members may have advocated for the client to be allowed to remain in the program. Strong advocacy from a staff member could keep a client in the program, at least for a while longer. If the staff members felt sufficiently strong, they could, in effect, veto the removal decision of the other staff because the other staff would respect the sentiments of the still-hopeful colleague.

For example, after being in the program for ten months, Robbie was considered by Mitch and the counselors to likely graduate in a few months. However, he began to miss drug tests and treatment sessions. Mitch suspected that Robbie was using and would skip treatment sessions in order to avoid the drug test. Alice, the lead counselor, thought Robbie was using but held out hope for him due to his having confessed to using drugs many months earlier–a good sign–and his later months of being clean, plus his previous active participation in treatment. Several times she talked Mitch out of a removal recommendation by asking for another chance for Robbie.

Suspecting that a colleague may propose removing a client, a staff member may preempt that possibility. In the following staffing, Jane, a counselor, knowing that Aaron, a client, had tested positive again for using cocaine, feared that Mitch would seek to remove Aaron from the program. Jane began the discussion by casting the client's most recent positive drug test as a "teachable moment." She also made other claims for the client that presented the rule violation as less negative than it might otherwise have been interpreted.

> "I think we might have a teachable moment with Aaron," Jane opened. "He tested positive for cocaine and that caught him off guard." She continued, "He just ran into an old dealer of his. The guy said he hadn't seen Aaron around much and that he had some killer stuff. Aaron immediately bought and used some. He is truly upset that people don't see him as he sees himself. Aaron sees himself as a caring guy and others see him as not giving a sh-t. He picked the three strongest people in group to give him feedback and they all told him the same thing (which Mitch understood as the three clients were brutally honest with Aaron) . . . For some reason it is real important to him that he complete drug court. He needs to complete something that is really hard."

Jane had not lost hope in Aaron. She understood the client's drug use as an opportunity for change. She implicitly characterized him as motivated to finish drug court. She supported this view by noting that the client picked the three most direct members of group to provide feedback. Her advocacy made the discussion of removal inappropriate.

Trials

As professional staff in the three drug courts we studied lost hope, they typically did not immediately recommend to the judge that the unworthy clients be dismissed from the program. Instead, staff provided opportunities to the clients to show that the clients could and would comply with the requirements of the program, and, therefore, the staff should remain hopeful and allow the clients to continue in the program. Trials reflected the desire of staff to help drug-using offenders go straight and to assure themselves that they had indeed given the offenders a fair chance to perform satisfactorily in the program. Trials reflected and supported the professional image the staff had for themselves and for what they did. Ranging from the least to the most definitive were three kinds of trials: *warnings, last-chance agreements* and *judge's threats.*

In warnings, staff told clients that they were headed for removal if they did not begin to comply with program requirements. Judges, treatment staff, or program coordinators warned clients in court, by telephone, in an office or during a counseling session. Warnings could be general or include specific requirements to be met such as "no more missed appointments; even if you are dead, you'd better be there" or "you have reached the end of the line; no more dirty tests; you'd better get it together." Judges warned clients heading for removal and at times told them to see their counselors to learn what they needed to do to stay in the program.

Consider Robert, who had been a client in the drug court program in Urban County several months. He had previously tested positive four times for marijuana and once for cocaine and denied use for his most recent positive test, claiming that his positive drug test was due to inhaling secondary marijuana smoke as he took a car trip to the coast. He attended counseling sessions irregularly. After court, Mitch told Robert that he needed to stay away from his friends and his uncles.

Compare the private, word-to-the-wise warning Mitch gave Robert with the public warning Mitch gave Greg in court. Greg had been in the program a little more than five months, with periods of great participation and periods of lousy performance. Greg had not violated program requirements in several months, but he did not speak in counseling sessions and was viewed by staff as unmotivated.

> Your honor, I would like to call Greg. If Greg continues his current patterns, he will never graduate the program. He does great for about a month or a month and a half, then he messes up. He fails a drug test, which is the most common way he messes up. If he never makes a change, he will never graduate drug court. He could be here for ten years, everyone in this room could go away, and he still would not graduate.

Staff warned clients whom they believed could comply with program requirements but were not participating properly in drug court. Staff warned clients in order to elicit greater external motivation from the clients, which staff hoped would become internal motivation.

In the early years of Urban County's drug court, Mitch and the other professional staff frequently used last-chance agreements, sometimes called "thirty-day contracts." The last-chance agreement was a form filled in by treatment staff and enforced by Mitch that notified clients they had one last chance to follow the requirements of the program. Clients signed the last-chance agreement, acknowledging that any future rule violation would lead to removal.

In the following case summary, Danny, a client who had done poorly in the program, was given a last chance contract. Staff characterized him as "treatment wise." The client could say the right treatment words, but his behavior remained unchanged.

> Danny was admitted to services on 10/25 and has attended five of six groups, three of three UAs. Client stalled on all UAs on 11/20. He was in the bathroom stall for over two hours and staff recorded his failure to deliver a sample as a positive. Danny has a long history of manipulative behavior. Client in group and homework assignments reflects "treatment smarts" and not an application of basic recovery ideas. Danny's progress is completely unsatisfactory. Client's group participation is characterized by excuses, rationalizations, and justifications for his willful behavior. Recommendation is for a two-week last chance agreement; if there is no significant improvement in two weeks, recommen-

dation will be for removal.

The last-chance agreement notified Danny that either he change his behavior or the treatment staff would recommend removal. Failing a last chance agreement did not guarantee removal but was a gravely serious strike. Danny survived in the program for a few more weeks before he was removed.

Finally, judges occasionally threatened clients that if they did not comply with a specific, named requirement, such as missing no more counseling sessions or changing their friends, then the clients would definitely be removed from the program.[3]

Robbie, who we discussed earlier, always tested positive as graduation approached. Mitch told the judge in the pre-court meeting of their suspicions of his using drugs and their plan to test him (and several other clients before court). The pre-court meeting ended early and Mitch went to test Robbie. Robbie claimed that he could not urinate, that he had just done so before court, and that that he could not possibly do so again. "Ask anyone, I just peed," he remarked. Mitch "knew" that Robbie was dodging the drug test as the body produces urine in about twenty minutes. In court, Mitch reported that Robbie could not "deliver a sample." The judge chastised him and told him to report to Mitch at 8:30 the next morning. "If you can't give a sample then, you are out," the judge threatened Robbie. Off to the side, the judge told Mitch that if Robbie tested positive, he was out of the program.

The public nature of the judge's threat to remove Robbie if he did not produce a urine sample the next morning bound the judge, at least to some degree, to carry out that threat. How would the judge look to the staff and the drug court clients if he did not back up his threats? While the judge's statement to Mitch to remove Robbie if he tested positive was not made as publicly as the threat to Robbie, it still bound the judge's actions. The next day, Robbie tested dirty. His parents came to the following court session to plead for another chance for their son. No drug court professional supported the parents' plea, and the judge did not grant it.[4]

---

3. A judge may threaten a specific client or mark a policy change through a general threat. For example, one judge announced that any client caught faking a urine sample would automatically be removed.
4. Judges' "threats" were based, at least in part, on the reasoning that clients had control over their behavior, believed the judges, were aware of the consequences, and were capable of

Trials provided opportunities for clients for whom staff members were losing hope to comply with program requirements and to forestall their removal from the program. Clients who passed the trials remained in the program, having further opportunities to perform successfully and redeem themselves in the judgment of the staff. Clients who failed the tests confirmed the staff's judgment of their lack of worth. They were removed.

Reviewing the Record

As professional staff came to decide to remove a client from drug court, the program coordinator in all three counties reviewed the client's record, listing the client's violations of the program's requirements. The coordinator often did this after warnings had been issued and last-chance contracts imposed. Through a review of the record, the coordinator built a case for the client's removal that would be presented to the judge, much as staffers do in other service or court agencies when removing clients or closing cases (Higgins, 1985; Holstein, 1993). The record review provided a simple, potentially powerful, indictment of the client as someone who was unworthy of continuing in the program.

Mitch listed the following record review on a piece of paper to prepare for the removal of a client:

- Right before a surprise test he admitted to using drugs.
- 3rd positive test
- Put on probation during last court
- Fails to complete assignments

Mitch judged the three positive tests to be the least significant failures in the record review. The failure to complete assignments was a more important concern as it showed inadequate motivation. The client was making insufficient effort in treatment to change. That the

---

making rational choices. We are unsure as to whether all four conditions were always present when threats to remove clients were made and kept. The judge in Farming County's drug court announced in court that any client forging documents showing they attend self-help groups would be removed from the program. Within a week, the counselor caught Billy, a client, forging attendance documentation. Billy had been doing well in the program, and Mitch believed that eventually he would graduate. At the next court session, Billy admitted that he forged the attendance slip and explained that because he had been working a lot recently, he did not have time to attend the self-help meeting. The judge removed him. For months afterward, the judge and Mitch discussed the client's removal.

client had been put on probation was a reminder to the judge and others that a last-chance agreement had been set and the client had failed to abide by it.[5]

Mitch used the record review at times to guide his discussion with treatment providers to remove clients. He used it to make a case in court to remove clients. Professional staff and judges accepted the record review as an accurate depiction of the client. However, at times, through the record review, Mitch and other staff decided that clients who were moving toward removal were not as unworthy, not as hopeless, as their staff discussions had suggested. These clients were allowed to remain in the program.

Presenting the Case for Removal

The final, often dramatic, step in removing a client from the program was the presentation in court of the case for removal. Through presenting the case, the coordinator intended to convince the judge to remove the client or provide additional support to the judge's earlier agreement to the recommendation to remove the client. Finally, presenting the case served to instruct the other drug court clients sitting in court of what could happen to them if they performed inadequately in the program. In the courtroom, recommendations for removal shifted from their planning to performance.

Presenting the case for the client's removal likely appeared to the casual observer as an attack on the client by the staff (Garfinkel, 1956). When presenting a case in court for a client's removal, Mitch did not try to present an impartial account of the client's participation in drug court. Instead, he attempted to build a compelling case that the unworthy client must be removed. The client's failures were highlighted. The client would not and could not change. No further effort from the program was warranted.

In the following presentation, Mitch called Joe, the client, to stand before the judge, reciting Joe's failures in the program and publicly pushing the judge to remove him.

> *Mitch:* Your honor, the client attended five for five sessions, one UA, positive for cocaine on November 4th. Client admitted to using on

5. A brief record review, as in the above example, does not mean a weak case for removal. Drug court professionals attended to offenders in terms of drug-court relevant behaviors and attitudes.

November 3rd, but continued to blame use on something else. Client was confronted on his repeated failure to humble himself and let go of self-will. Client continues to portray the pitiful person after his drug use but fails to learn from his repeated use. Much time is taken away from others to assist the client, who fails to help himself. Recommendation is discharge. How long have we stood by Joe and he has let us down? Not once has Joe accepted responsibility for his action. He always has an excuse or story.

Joe: I know I have done wrong, your honor. I thought I had this thing beat. I made a mistake. If you could give me one more chance, I know I could do it this time.

Judge: Many times we have given you another chance.

Standing beside Joe was his mother who quietly wept. Joe was subdued and still. The judge looked at the mother and asked if she had anything to say.

Mother: Please, judge, let Joe have one more chance. He is a good boy and I know he can do well in this program. Thank you. (Tears rolled down her face as she said this in a small voice.)

Judge: Joe, I don't know how many chances we have given you to straighten up. Now you want one more. Well, you have used them all up. I am going to order that you be removed from the program.

In his presentation to remove the client from the program, Mitch emphasized that Joe gave excuses for his failures instead of accepting responsibility for his willful violations of program requirements and learning from them. Mitch portrayed Joe as the unworthy criminal who no longer deserved to be in drug court.

In response to this presentation of the client as a willful failure, Joe only requested another chance. He did not dispute the portrayal nor try to recast his dismal participation in the program with an alternative explanation. Joe responded weakly to Mitch's characterization of him as unworthy. Joe's ally, his mother, could have been an advantage. However, the mother's tears, while sad, did not effectively contest the professional's portrayal of her son. Had she presented herself as a strong individual who intended to actively help Joe, perhaps some hope awaited them. However, she seemed resigned to her son's fate. The judge removed Joe.

GRADUATING FROM DRUG COURT

Graduations from drug court were public, exciting, and emotional ceremonies. Like all public ceremonies, decisions and plans that were neither public nor visible to outsiders led to graduations. Compared to removing clients from drug court, graduation from drug court almost followed from the uneventful participation of clients in drug court. It was the expected outcome of compliance. Staff, however, could justify graduation on two conditions, including a sense of obligation given the client's compliance and a staff member's deep belief that the client had made significant life changes.

Some clients who graduated from drug court were in compliance during their entire participation in the program. In the three courts we studied, clients who graduated may have progressed from a "good start" to "doing well" to "showing leadership" to graduation. "Boring clients," Mitch kidded with clients, was what he wanted. Boring clients were compliant with all program regulations at the time of graduation. Other clients made dramatic changes in their actions while participating, having failed several drug tests earlier in the program and struggling to open up in counseling. While none of the three drug courts that we examined had set rules about the necessary length of complete compliance before clients could graduate, Mitch has observed programs that required complete compliance for twelve weeks to five months before clients were allowed to graduate.

In the following, we first discuss the graduation criteria used by program staff to decide who would graduate. Next, we examine the process through which the professional staff decided clients would graduate. Finally, we present the graduation, an emotional ceremony in which the clients leave drug court with honor and praise.

Graduation Criteria

From the treatment perspective of assisting drug users to become drug free, graduation was intended for clients who had achieved all of their treatment goals and who had complied with all program requirements. At a minimum, clients had to have regularly attended counseling sessions, paid their fees, attended self-help meetings, made treatment progress, and achieved a long record of clean drug tests. No formally stated minimum length of time for complete compliance existed in the three courts we studied, though staff expected complete compliance for many weeks preceding graduation. Clients could not become completely compliant in the "twenty-third hour" and graduate in the "next hour."

The length of stay in drug court for those who graduated varied among the three courts. In Farming County's drug court, clients must have participated in the program a minimum of fifty-two weeks, though a few exceptions were made. The length of the client's participation in the program was less fixed in the other two courts. The average length of stay for those who graduated approached two years in Suburban County's drug court and fourteen months in Urban County's drug court. The differences in program length are due to different treatment providers with different philosophies.[6]

In the courts we studied, staff fundamentally decided that graduation was appropriate when the clients had met their treatment goals. Treatment staff wrote goals for every client, though seldom shared them with other staff. On a few occasions, staff judged that clients had made sufficient progress to graduate even though not all treatment goals had been met. In these cases, staff had written long-term goals for the clients that went beyond the expectations for what was to be achieved in drug court.[7]

In the drug courts in Suburban and Urban counties, the treatment staff devised a test, a series of questions, given to clients to aid in deciding whether clients would be promoted a phase within the program or graduate. The staff used the questions to learn what the clients understood about the recovery process, based on the material offered in the treatment program. The tests, however, did not determine whether clients graduated. Staff typically reasoned that treatment for clients was complete when they had regularly attended self-help meetings in the community and had a series of negative drug tests.

Mitch felt obligated to allow clients to graduate when they showed achievement on the five dimensions of treatment progress: attendance at counseling sessions and other required activities, drug testing, pay-

---

6. Drug courts elsewhere used different, sometimes more formal, procedures for deciding who met graduation criteria. For example, the drug court in Oakland, California, used a point system based on rewards, punishments, and client behaviors. Clients graduated when they earned a set number of points (Bedrick & Skolnick, 1999).

7. We have no specific examples of treatment goals since this material was confidential and not available to non-treatment staff. A common alcohol and other drug treatment goal might be, "List and discuss ways in which drug use had caused your family pain."

ment of fees, participation in self-help meetings, and treatment progress. Even when he had suspicions, though not proof, he felt obligated to graduate the clients.

Ray, a young single male who was arrested for PWID marijuana and who graduated from Farming County's drug court, was rumored to have been falsifying his urine tests and to have been continuing to use drugs on a limited basis. The staff, however, did not catch him breaking any rules. After he graduated, another client in the group told the staff that Ray had continued to use drugs during the program. He used very little and only on specific days so as to avoid testing positive according to the other group member. Mitch told the other staff in Farming County's drug court program that he felt legally obligated to allow Ray to graduate. Evidence of program violations, not rumors, was needed to keep clients from graduating, Mitch believed.

Several months after Ray graduated from drug court, police arrested him on drug charges. Ray's rearrest supported a staff belief that even if clients deceptively completed the program without making real changes in themselves, they would eventually be caught and "pay the price." This reasoning by staff enabled them with somewhat fewer misgivings to allow dubious clients to graduate.

The Graduation Process

Graduation, a joyous, public ceremony, was the culmination of the graduation process. Through the two-step process of broaching the possibility of graduation to fellow drug court professionals and then announcing in court the upcoming graduation, staff moved clients toward graduation. Staff members brought up with their colleagues the possibility of graduation for a client. They broached the topic. When other staff supported the client's graduation, the next step was the announcement. Typically, the judge made the announcement in court that a client would graduate in several weeks or on a specific date if the client continued to participate successfully.

Broaching the Graduation

Treatment staff or program coordinators could broach the possibility of graduation for a client. When Mitch broached the possibility, he often did so in order that a treatment slot became available for an offender waiting to enter drug court. More frequently, treatment staff initiated the graduation process.

When staff or coordinators broached the possibility of graduation, one of several outcomes might occur: acceptance, negotiation, or rejection. When the possibility of graduation was broached, other staff may agree. In the following, Alice, a treatment counselor in Urban County drug court, mentioned to Mitch and the other counselors that some clients could graduate in the future. Alice's colleagues agreed with her, which suggested that the staff saw graduation for those clients as approaching certainty:

> *Alice:* What about Andrew graduating?
> *Mitch:* What do you think?
> *Alice:* He has done a whole lot of work.
> *Mitch:* I think that is great, and I do not have any problem with him graduating. I wish he were someone we could keep hold of because he had done so well.

Mitch met the counselor's suggestion of the client's graduation with encouragement. The counselor supported her suggestion through her comment that the client had "done a whole lot of work." This showed he was worthy to graduate. Mitch's playful comment that he wished the program could keep him showed that he supported without reservation the client's graduation. However, staff did not always accept the suggestion that a client graduate.

At times, staff members were hesitant to graduate a client when a colleague broached the possibility. Instead, they might negotiate an arrangement. For example, Mitch broached the possibility of graduation for Teddy, a client who had been in the Farming County drug court program for forty-three weeks. The judge and counselor commented that the client had not been in the program for one year. Mitch negotiated with the judge and counselor, the three deciding that forty-seven weeks of participation would be sufficient for the client to graduate.

At times when the client's graduation was broached, other staff rejected the possibility. Rejection was sufficient to delay graduation. The most frequent reason given by staff for delaying rejections was that the client needed a few more weeks or another month of treatment before being ready to graduate and to live without the program. Mitch was generally supportive of the counselors' claims.[8]

---

8. In the early years of Urban County's drug court, Mitch interviewed former clients a few

Graduation Announcement

Once staff agreed upon graduation for clients, they or the judge announced it to the clients and the others in the group. Counselors told clients in group counseling that the staff would recommend to the judge that they soon graduate. When the announcement occurred in court, the judge made it. In Farming County, the drug court judge often told the clients, "Well, you won't be with us much longer." In most announcements, staff and judges encouraged and cautioned the clients. They cautioned clients in order to motivate them to continue to participate successfully in the program and not to backslide.

In the following, Mitch announced to the courtroom that three clients could soon graduate. The judge congratulated and cautioned them:

> Mitch said to the judge and the entire courtroom, "Let me call then Mr. Droon, Mr. Demm, and Mr. Henry." As they walked to the front of the court, he continued, "All three could graduate in six weeks." At this, the drug court clients and others in the courtroom applauded.
>
> The judge remarked, "Gentlemen, congratulations to all three of you. That is a wonderful thing to look forward to. The only thing I always tell folks when they near graduation is this is the time not to let down, keep it up. You have come this far. You do not want anything to happen near the end. You want to be ready to celebrate that moment, and we want to celebrate it with you. I congratulate your accomplishments to this point."

Note the judge's warning to the three clients to not "let down." This can be understood as friendly advice from a judge who is concerned for the clients' welfare. It can also be understood as an assertion of the court's jurisdiction over the clients and their legal obligation to comply. Implicit in the warning is that failure to participate adequately in the remaining weeks would jeopardize graduation.

---

months after they graduated from the program. He learned that graduates look forward to leaving the program but they were often concerned about being on their own. Drug tests and meetings gave clients stong incentives not to use. These external constraints were lost when clients graduated. They had to rely on themselves–as well as on support in the community, including self-help groups. This concern of clients led staff to implement a procedure for over a year in which counselors gave clients approved for graduation a month off from the program and then brought them back for a few more group sessions. This experimental procedure slowed the graduation process but gave the clients more time to learn to care for themselves.

Graduation

Graduation was a semi-ceremony that the professional staff gladly anticipated. Speeches, however brief, were made, glad sentiments were offered, feelings of hard-earned accomplishment were felt, and tears were sometimes shed.[9]

Graduation consisted of four elements: a brief statement from the program coordinator praising the graduating client; formal recognition from the judge and the court; a brief speech from the client, and applause from those in attendance. Program coordinators or sometimes treatment counselors praised the accomplishments of the graduating clients through brief, often humorous, stories about the clients. At times, the coordinators' statements included a comparison of pre- and post-drug court behavior of the clients or a morality play in which, through hard work and perhaps some setbacks, the worthy drug users had redeemed their lives.

In Suburban County's drug court, the counselor stood and told the court how he thought one graduating client would never get through the program because he was such a "knucklehead." As the counselor talked, he became quite emotional and shed a few tears over the client's accomplishments.

In all three courts studied, the judge left the bench to shake the graduates' hands. Certificates of graduation were also presented in all three courts. In Suburban County's drug court, small tokens, including self-help recovery books, were given. In Urban County's drug court, Mitch developed over the time the phrase, "It is the recommendation of the prosecuting attorney's office that since (client's name) has met all the requirements of the program that he or she graduate the program and all charges against him or her be dismissed." Mitch spoke this statement with a degree of formality and earnestness. He believed it sounded official, like a decree.

---

9. Graduation is typically the last time drug court staff saw or talked with graduated clients. On rare occasions, counselors or program coordinators may encounter former clients in the community. Occasionally former clients called or stopped by to tell Mitch how they were doing after leaving drug court. One graduated client called Mitch about every six months for more than five years. Mitch and other staff always found it gratifying to learn how former clients were continuing to improve their lives. A few who were removed from the program even told Mitch how their removal was the beginning of their recovery. As one former client remarked, "If I couldn't make it in drug court, I knew I had a problem." In a few cases, counselors and coordinators encountered former graduates or participants when they were rearrested. Sometimes Mitch spoke with the prosecutor on their behalf.

Graduates made speeches after being recognized by the court. However lengthy or short the speech, the graduates invariably thanked the program and often the counselors for helping them. Infrequently they mentioned Mitch, whom they saw much less frequently than they saw the counselors and with whom they interacted less intensely than they did with the counselors once they were in the program.

The audience always applauded the graduates. Sometimes, audience members stood and commented aloud to the graduates. This occurred frequently in Suburban County's drug court. When audience members spoke, they often wished the graduate good luck or briefly remarked how the program had helped the graduate. When a client named Willie graduated, the audience started yelling "Free Willie" repeatedly, a humorous take-off of the movie by the same name.

Frequently family members, including parents, children, siblings, aunts and uncles, accompanied the graduating client to graduation. At times, family members, especially mothers, accompanied the graduate at the front of the courtroom. The judges often encouraged the family members to say a few words. The mothers' remarks expressed their appreciation for what drug court provided their children and pride in their children's accomplishments.

The following is a typical graduation moment in Urban County's drug court:

> *Mitch:* Your honor, that concludes the reports. We have five people graduating. I would like to call Mr. Sam Droon first. I can tell you, your honor, that for many years Mr. Droon had the most dangerous job in the world. He was a fisherman off the coast of Florida. He had an elaborate system. He would go to sea to dry out. Then he would come back to land to get high until he ran out of money. Then he would go back to sea. Maybe he thought he could do a little better. What the staff tells me is that right from the start he took hold of the program. He came in regularly to the groups; he was regular at work and never tested positive. That was very unusual, very unusual. It is the recommendation of the prosecuting attorney's office that since Mr. Droon has met all the requirements of the program, he graduate the program and all charges against him be dismissed.
>
> *Judge:* You must be proud of yourself. This is quite an accomplishment. This certificate says that you are Mr. Sam Droon and that you graduated the Urban County drug court program.

(Audience applause.)
Mitch: Your honor it is a requirement of the program that the graduate address the audience.
Judge: Well, if you like to, go ahead.
Sam: I don't really have much to say. I want to thank all of you. I have come a long way. I just want to thank God.
(Audience applause.)

CONCLUSION

Through judging the performance of drug court clients and upon staff recommendation, drug court judges removed or graduated drug court clients. The unworthy criminal was kicked out. The worthy drug user who had gone straight graduated. Occasionally, judges deferred the decision in order to allow the clients to participate further in drug court with the hope that the client would graduate. Removal and graduation were the culmination of months, even a couple of years, of drug court.

When drug court staff admitted drug-using offenders to drug court, they experienced hope that the program would enable the drug users to become drug and crime free. The worthy clients had potential to succeed. As the clients participated in drug court, staff provided services, monitored their participation, and sanctioned their conduct. Were the clients motivated? Were they learning and applying their tools? Were they staying drug free? As the clients' participation continued, the staff judged their performance. Were the clients' performance worthy of graduation? Or, had clients violated program regulations and expectations such that staff began to and eventually lost hope? Had the worthy admission become the unworthy criminal to be removed? The joy of graduation, however, enabled the drug court staff to experience less painfully the loss of hope.

In order to enable drug-using offenders to become drug free and, thereby, to become law-abiding citizens whose lives had turned around, drug court professionals judged the drug users. They judged potential, participation and performance. They judged the worth of people who came before them as drug-using offenders to be admitted, promoted or held them back during treatment, and removed or graduated them from drug court. In judging drug users, the drug court professionals gave the individuals before them moral identities of varying worth. Graduation made their job worthwhile.

EPILOGUE

America, like all societies, defines its citizens' drug use and identifies its drug users. It, like all societies, creates in at least one important sense the drug problems it experiences. It defines and responds to some drug use as a problem, as a phenomenon to be controlled because it is harmful to society. Other drug use it has accepted or even promoted. America has defined and redefined the same drug in various ways such as in the country's shifting responses to tobacco from heavily subsidizing and promoting the use of the commodity to extracting billions of dollars from the tobacco industry for the harm it has caused the country (Gately, 2001). Through national, state and even local debate, legislation and response, America has defined its citizen's drug use. In Chapter 1, we highlighted some features of the country's ongoing drug policy. For more than one hundred years, America's drug policy has been a shifting combination of treatment and punishment toward the users of various drugs.

In responding to drug use defined as problematic, America has also identified its drug users. It has given its problem drug users the identities they are assumed to have. As presented in the Introduction, the typical understanding is that people have inside of them their "who-they-are"–their selves. Given their biological inheritance and development over the course of their lives in interaction with others, people develop their selves. Who people are "resides" inside of them, a coherent self. Another approach is that observers give identities to the people they encounter. Observers attribute characteristics to people as part of making sense of their experiences with others. While identification, the giving of identities to others, occurs when people interact with each other, it also occurs when observers address an entire category of people. The observers characterize or give an identity to that category of others. Who are those others? What are they like? What are their motivations? What can be expected of them? Through identification, observers are making meaningful the others and telling themselves how to handle the others. America has done that with its problem drug users.

In the following, we summarize the main points we developed throughout the book about the construction of moral identity in drug court. Next we emphasize that drug courts and their staff produce the successes and failures they experience. In so doing, we stress the value of studying what the staff does, including what the staff does in problem-solving courts. We end by commenting on critics' concerns that drug courts, steeped in therapeutic jurisprudence, do not adequately safeguard the due process rights of the drug court clients.

CONSTRUCTING DRUG OFFENDERS' IDENTITIES

America has given problem drug users varied and shifting identities from troubled, even pitiful abusers and addicts who need help to crazed junkies and sociopathic criminals who threaten the safety of law-abiding citizens and their communities. The tension between identifying problem drug users as worthy abusers and addicts and as unworthy deviants and criminals has marked America's response to problem drug use for more than a century. Drug court has arisen from and reflects that identity tension.

Drug courts, as we explained in Chapter 1, developed to help the criminal justice system handle the surging increase in drug cases that began in the middle 1980s with the growing use of cocaine and later crack. Drug courts were intended to help the worthy addicts who committed crimes due to their addiction to become sober and crime-free. Through their policies and practices, drug courts decide who are worthy addicts and who are not. As these policies and practices vary throughout the country, who are identified as worthy addicts and who are not varies too.

The drug courts that we studied, like many drug courts, judged the potential, participation and performance of the drug-using offenders who became their applicants, clients, successes and failures. When judging potential, the drug court staff and the judges who preside over drug court decided whether the drug-using offenders had a significant drug problem, were motivated to become sober, had the capacity to participate successfully in the program, and did not pose an unacceptable risk to the program. However, the staff and judges assumed that they could never be certain about their decisions, about who would succeed or fail. They also operated with the disposition that within their policy guidelines and available resources, they would give a chance to those for whom they had at least some hope. Supporters of the drug users, such as their family and their lawyers who advocated for the drug users' admission, could increase the likelihood that staff would have hope that the drug users would participate successfully in the program. Staff did not target those who were recreational drug users with no serious criminal history. Had they done so, they could have achieved a higher success rate than they did. Neither did they accept drug users with a significantly violent criminal history. Had they done so, they may have jeopardized support for their programs. In judging potential as they did, the three drug courts that we studied began to produce the successes and failures that they would later experience and record.

As clients participated in the drug court programs, the staff provided services and monitored the clients' progress. The staff decided who in the group sessions were working to understand and manage their drug use and who were playing games; whose positive test for drug use indicated the intentional use of drugs to get high and whose did not and, therefore, who lied or told the truth when confronted with positive tests for drug use; and whose absence from group was acceptable and whose was not. The staff interpreted clients' behaviors such as testing negative for drug use or failing to attend group counseling as signs of where the clients were potentially headed. They developed folk explanations for clients' inappropriate behavior, such as interpreting a male client's drug use as due to his being steered wrong by a female friend. As the staff interacted with the clients over months, they increasingly came to identify clients as criminal, slick, a leader, someone working hard or stepping up or with other characterizations that indicated that they were worthy drug users committed to becoming sober or were unworthy criminals trying to fool the staff into believing otherwise or so little concerned to even try to do that. The staff typically concerned themselves more with clients they defined as problems and identified them with more evocative terms compared to clients who were seen as progressing uneventfully through the program. As the staff variously identified clients, they were preparing themselves for deciding whether to graduate the clients or remove them from the program.

With the continued participation of the clients, the staff judged the clients' performance. The staff began to lose hope that some clients would successfully complete the program. When they did, they provided trials to the clients, a final opportunity for clients to show that they could meet the requirements of the program. Trials were also a means for staff to assure themselves that they had given clients every opportunity to succeed in the program. Staff typically removed those who failed the trials. The staff judged those clients to be unworthy of further assistance from the program. As the "leaders," the ones "working hard," and the other clients who were progressing through the phases of the program neared what the staff understood to be the completion of the program, the staff signaled these clients that they soon would graduate. Within the policies of the drug court programs, the staff and judges decided who succeeded and who failed. The drug court staff identified the drug users they encountered, giving them identities as more or less worthy users as they accepted or rejected applicants, as they served and monitored the progress of clients, and as they removed or graduated clients from the program.

The drug users who appear in drug court could be understood as being richly complex people, as could all individuals. However, drug court professionals construct organizationally relevant identities for drug users. The professionals identify the drug users through a much smaller number of drug-court relevant traits. Drug court professionals' construction of the moral identities of people who use drugs is embedded within their courts' policies. The policies, in turn, respond to the concerns and debate about drugs that occur from the local to the national level.

PRODUCING SUCCESSES AND FAILURES

Drug courts produce the successes and failures and all their other outcomes, which staff, evaluators, and other observers of the courts may too quickly attribute to the conduct and characteristics of the drug users. Of course, drug courts do this as they work with drug users who behave in various ways, but the behavior of the drug users does not itself decide the outcomes. The staff does (Higgins, 1998). For example, drug court clients do not fail the program, though that is typically how staff understands what has happened when they remove the clients from the program. Clients may have tested positive for illicit drug use, not paid court costs, not attended group counseling, and even committed new crimes. However, those behaviors do not remove them from the program. Staff often accept, even expect, clients to behave in such ways. The staff and judges remove the clients from the program. That may seem obvious, but the importance of the obvious may sometimes be overlooked. Within their courts' policies, through their evaluations of the clients, in light of the resources available and the potential clients waiting to enter, and through interaction with each other, the staff and judges produce the failures–and successes–of the clients. Insiders and outsiders may agree that how staff and judges produce the failures and the successes is reasonable, effective, timely, and so forth. Or the insiders and outsiders may disagree. But whether they agree or not on the policies and practices of drug courts and their staff, they and we should not mistake the target of the staff's actions for the cause of their decisions.

As drug courts and staff change their policies, procedures, evaluations, and decisions, they will change the successes and failures they produce. For example, we should expect that, with all else the same, those drug courts mandated to take all drug-using offenders would have a lower rate of success than those courts that have discretion in who they accept. Or, we should expect, with all else the same, those drug courts that do not allow their clients to have setbacks, such as consuming drugs while in the program, will have a lower rate of success than those courts that assume setbacks will occur.

Similarly, if one staff member believes a particular client is superficially complying to get through the program without making any significant change and other staff members feel differently, the first staff member will likely make different recommendations regarding the client than the others do. Client behavior will likewise be differently interpreted. A missed appointment could be a sign of an unreliable car or continued manipulation, depending on the staff. Depending on how staff members manage their differences, the client may be kept in the program or removed. When the staff's professional perspectives and practices differ, they may handle drug offenders in importantly different ways, producing different outcomes.

Since staff, including the judge, produce the successes and failures of drug court as they manage drug-using offenders through interaction with the offenders and with their colleagues and within the policies and procedures of their courts, we encourage students of drug courts to explore carefully what staff do and why. With the increasing emphasis on entering the "black box" of drug treatment, it is important to attend to staff. Our work has been a start at doing that. No matter how well conducted, evaluation studies and discussions about drug court as a system will not be adequate if the working of drug court is not understood. The staff and the drug-using offenders do that work.

With the rise of therapeutic jurisprudence has come the development of other specialty courts that handle problematic behavior including domestic violence, mental illness, drunk driving, gambling, homelessness, truancy and gun possession. The limited research and thinking about these problem-solving courts, as they have been about drug courts, focus on the general design of the courts, evaluation of the effectiveness of the courts, and the outcomes of clients with varying characteristics. The research and discussion have largely overlooked the work of the staff in these problem-solving courts. Yet, working within their organization's policies and procedures and in interaction with each other and with applicants and clients, staff members produce the outcomes of these problem-solving courts that the evaluation research attempts to predict and observers attempt to understand (Berman & Feinblatt, 2005). How staff members in these other problem-solving courts do so should appropriately concern us.

CONCLUSION

Critics of therapeutic jurisprudence, a foundation of drug court, have raised concerns about drug court. As we presented in Chapter 1, some have criticized the intrusion of a growing "therapeutic culture" in America into drug court (Nolan, 1998, 2001). This therapeutic intrusion allows for the courts to exercise increased control over the client's self as well as body, presumably for the good of the client.

One of the consequences of such increased control, critics caution, is inadequate attention to the client's due process rights. For example, since drug court is to be nonadversarial, the client loses the defense of his or her attorney. However, the good intentions of the staff do not compensate for a strong legal defense. Or, in traditional courts, urine testing can only occur if ordered by the court. A chain of custody must be maintained, and the defense is free to challenge the results. In drug court, at least in the three we studied, none of this occurs; these due process rights are waived. The critics' concerns are important.

Counterpoised to the critics' concerns, at least in the three drug courts we studied, is how the courts and the staff operated. Those admitted into the three drug courts we studied were the "dead-bang guilty." Their lawyers did not believe they were innocent. Neither did the offenders. The offenders had committed the crime, were drug users and needed help. The drug court clients voluntarily participated. While participating, some used drugs as indicated by their drug tests. They were not arrested, charged with a new offense, and removed from the program–at least not with their early use. Instead, they continued in the program and many graduated. Many graduates appreciated the opportunity drug court provided for them to become sober, to straighten out their lives.

Through a close look at how drug court staff and judges operate within drug court, we can better assess the concerns of the critics. In the courts we studied, those concerns, we believe, were counterbalanced by the reluctance of the staff to give up on the drug users. Staff lost hope after clients were understood to have violated the program requirements numerous times.

Drug courts do rely on the good intentions and knowledge of professional staff to avoid legal abuse. The staff we observed strove to help drug-using offenders. They were experienced professionals. Good intentions, however, may serve as justification for practices that are harsher than what the drug-using offenders would be subject to within criminal court. Misunderstandings may lead to legal consequences that should not have happened.

For example, punishment that may have been excessive compared to what would have been received had the offender remained within criminal court was recommended several times during our study. One treatment counselor wanted to teach clients a lesson when they first tested positive for using drugs by sending the clients to jail for seventy-two hours. Other staff did not allow that to happen. Notice, however, that even in these instances, one staff member's intentions were reigned in by the other staff.

Or, consider that staff and judges at times interpreted the results of drug tests that were at odds with the scientific understanding of how the drug tests should be interpreted. As we mentioned in Chapter 4, staff and judges interpreted a change in a levels test from one administration of the test to a subsequent administration as indicating a change in clients' drug use.[1] No scientific evidence supports such an interpretation. Nevertheless, judges sent clients to jail for twenty-four or forty-eight hours for using drugs based on a scientifically unsupported interpretation of drug test results.

The good intentions and professional competence of drug court staff do not guarantee that mistakes will not be made and that the legal rights of offenders may not always be upheld. However, we should not overlook that mistakes and failure to uphold legal rights occur in criminal court, too. Perhaps more importantly, we should not forget that through dedication and competence and through working together within appropriate policies and procedures, drug court staffs throughout the country do tremendous good. They help drug-using offenders make more law-abiding and satisfying lives for themselves. In doing so, the drug court staffs help all of us.

Drug courts are a current development out of the more than century-long attempt of America and other countries to define and address their citizen's drug use and identify its drug users. The question has often been asked: Are problem drug users worthy addicts or unworthy criminals? The staff of drug court constantly faces that perplexing question as they judge drug users and create their moral identities.

---

1. Level tests report the number of nanograms of a drug metabolite per deciliter of body fluid. Such levels are affected by many things beyond drug use. For example, low fluid intake and outside work, like landscaping, would make the level go up since the overall fluid level is lowered and the drug metabolites remain constant.

Appendix

FIELD RESEARCHING DRUG COURT

Through more than five years of field research, we explored in three drug courts in a southeastern state how drug court staffers transformed drug-using offenders into drug court clients, some of whom succeeded and some of whom failed. Observing and talking with people as they participate in their social world and conduct their affairs are the foundation of field research. Field research may also include participating in the social world being explored as it did in our work. It is especially useful for the kind of social world that we investigated and for the questions that we acquired. Field research works well for investigating what occurs behind public scenes like most of the activities of drug court. It works well for trying to understand how members produce what occurs in their organization as they interact with each other, the members' perspectives that underlie their actions, and the members' experiences. These issues became the focus of our investigation of drug court. Trust between the investigators and the people whose worlds are investigated is important for creating understanding. Field research provides the opportunity to develop that trust. And even if not as much trust is created as the field researcher may wish, the researcher will still observe important, complex, often sensitive matters just by being present over a long time (Duneier, 1999; Jorgensen, 1989; Lofland & Lofland, 1995).

To help readers understand how we researched drug court, we briefly discuss the following matters: the drug courts and their locations, gaining approval, field roles and relations, ethics, observing and making notes, and analysis. A longer discussion is available elsewhere

(Mackinem, 2003b).

DRUG COURTS AND THEIR LOCATIONS

We observed in three adult drug courts in the metropolitan region of a state capital in a southeastern state. The drug courts were in three adjacent counties–Urban, Suburban, and Farming. We selected the drug courts because Mitch was the program coordinator in the drug courts in Urban and Farming counties and professionally knew staff in Suburban County's drug court. Mitch was the program coordinator in Urban County's drug court since it was established in fall 1996 until in 2004 when it was folded into Farming County's drug court, which was located in the same judicial circuit as Urban County. Urban County's drug court was closed and drug-using offenders from Urban County were required to travel to Farming County to participate in drug court. Urban County's drug court was closed in order to use its funding to maintain the drug court and treatment program for juveniles, which was established after the adult program and which lost its state funding. The Urban adult program reopened after a one and a half-year hiatus. Mitch served as the administrator in Farming County's drug court from its founding in 1998 to August 2005, when he left to take an academic position. We selected the drug court in Suburban County, which Mitch observed a handful of times from August 1997 to July 1999, because Mitch knew well the program director in that drug court and we wished to broaden our observations.

Urban County, whose drug court provided the majority of the observations that we made, is the location for the state capital and a large state university. The county is located in the middle of a state with great natural beauty but which economically and in quality-of-life matters such as health and well-being lags behind most other states. With professional, business, and white-collar employees living in Urban County, it recently had the third-highest average income among the state's counties. Almost half its residents are African-American, which is greater than the approximately 30 percent of the state's residents who are African-American.[1]

---

1. We mention this racial percentage and other location characteristics to provide the reader with a general feel for the types of communities involved, not because we use races as a way to make sense of drug court.

Rural Farming County, with agriculture and light industry, has an average income per worker of several thousand dollars less than Urban County. Approximately the same percentage of its residents is African-American as is the state's. West of Urban County is Suburban County, known as conservative and tough on crime. With many Suburban County residents driving to Urban County to work, it is comparably prosperous as is Urban County. However, compared to Urban and Farming counties, Suburban County has a significantly lower percentage of African-American residents, less than 15 percent.

The "typical" drug court client for the Urban and Farming counties, where most of the research was done, was an African-American male under the age of 30 who used crack cocaine.[2] From the beginning of these two drug courts until 2003, 61 percent of the 415 clients who entered the programs were African-American and 68 percent were male. Over one-third of the clients were between the ages of 22 and 30. Fifty-eight percent reported crack as their primary drug of choice. Nearly half spent more than $300 per week on drugs. Forty percent have graduated from drug court as compared to the national rate of 32 percent (Cooper, 2001).[3]

Mitch participated in and observed in three primary settings in drug court: offices, courtrooms, and jails. Offices of the treatment staff, prosecuting attorneys, public defenders, and program coordinators were the most common settings in which Mitch participated and observed.

---

2. Drug court clients varied among the three courts. In particular, drug court clients in Surburban County, based on the first four years of operation, were 55 percent white and 44 percent African-American. Forty-three percent of the clients in Suburban County's drug court used poweder cocaine as their primary drug of choice. However, we found no evidence in the cases that race or other common social characteristics played an overt role in staff's discussion.

3. Local arrest data for drug crimes did not include racial and gender breakdowns. Using state level arrest data, of those arrested for crack cocaine charges, African-American males compose 81 percent of arrests for serious crack cocaine drug crimes (including distribution, possession with intent and drug sale), as compared to only 6 percent for white males. Of those arrested for serious drug crimes, African-American males are nearly three times more likely to be arrested for serious drug crimes, beyond crack cocaine, than white males. However, when one includes less serious drug crimes for all drugs (including simple possession charge and possission of drug paraphernalia) this difference disappears, and, of those arrested, both racial groups are equally likely to be present. For all types of drugs, only 13 percent of females, of any race, were arrested for any serious drug crimes (including distribution, possession with intent and drug sale). The "typical" drug court client in our study does not match the statewide arrest data; females and white males are overrepresented in drug court. This variation is probably due to differences in the criminal history of drug users since none of the programs could take offenders with violent criminal convictions in their history. Further, all the programs studied avoided those charged with selling drugs.

Located in their respective county courthouses, Mitch's program coordinator's office in Urban County and the program coordinator's office in Suburban County contained computers, filing cabinets for case folders and functional, cost-effective furniture. Entering these two courthouses required passing through a metal detector staffed by police officers. Mitch had no office in the drug court program in Farming County. He squatted in available offices in the courthouse, which also served as the county services building.

Courtrooms are the most public setting for drug courts. The events of the Introduction to our book occurred in a courtroom in Urban County's judicial building. The courtrooms for Farming County's and Suburban County's drug court differed from each other and from the imposing courtroom used for drug court in Urban County. In Farming County, drug court was held in the basement of the county services building in a room that held fewer than forty people and was typically used for adjudicating misdemeanor cases. Off to one side of the judge's bench, a small platform behind a solid wood barrier, sat a small television used to show DUI arrest tapes. Suburban County's drug court was held in a courtroom that could seat 100 people and was adjacent to the county's jail. Judges occasionally commented to offenders that they could send the offenders through a small brown door that led directly to the jail.

Jails were the third important setting in which Mitch participated and observed. Program coordinators may go to jail to interview potential applicants for drug court. Until a new jail was built in Farming County, the previous jail was overcrowded; inmates slept in large dormitories with a wall of bars separating the dormitories from the halls; and no visitation, common or recreation rooms were available. Plaster fell from the ceiling. Mitch often met with offenders in the halls while other inmates walked by, mopped the floor or apparently wandered around. The new, modern jail in Farming County provided a room designed for visitation between lawyers and their clients where Mitch met with potential applicants. Mitch saw little of the jail in Suburban County as the drug court coordinator whom he accompanied met with potential applicants in the dining room after asking at the front desk to see them.

The jail in Urban County, the newest and largest of the three, housed approximately 1,200 inmates. Security was routinely tight. To meet with an inmate who was a potential applicant, Mitch passed through several locked doors and showed his ID to several officers in order to reach the housing units. At times of heightened security, Mitch was not allowed access to the housing units and met with potential applicants across a desk through a glass wall.

GAINING APPROVAL

Being a drug court program coordinator, having many years of experience as a drug counselor, and knowing some of the drug treatment providers eased Mitch's gaining approval to study the three drug courts. In the drug court programs in Urban and Farming Counties, Mitch mentioned his interest to his direct supervisor, a staff attorney, and then to the prosecuting attorney, who is the elected head of the prosecutor's office in the judicial circuit. After explaining his interest in developing an "insider understanding" of drug court, Mitch received explicit permission. Mitch received similar permission from the director of the treatment program and the staff and did so more than once as the treatment providers and staff changed. Mitch assured treatment staff that client information would be kept confidential. Identifying information such as race, age, and even gender would be altered if needed in order to protect the clients' identities. Seven of eight counselors representing the Urban and Farming courts treatment were receptive and interested. Knowing the coordinator of the drug court program and the director of the treatment program and several of the counselors professionally enabled Mitch to get permission to study Suburban County's drug court. In all three courts, the lawyers and treatment professionals were curious as to what Mitch planned to do. This book may answer their curiosity.

Early in the research, we decided that Mitch would not view the counseling sessions between the drug treatment staff and the drug court clients. Two considerations were important. First, alcohol and drug counseling is protected by strict laws of confidentiality. Second, Mitch's presence in the counseling sessions may have altered the sessions, especially given his authority as program coordinator who was involved in deciding who remained in the program and who graduated from the program. Through interviews with the counselors and through participating with the counselors in discussing and making decisions about the clients, Mitch was able to learn about the counselors' experiences and judgments. Unsolicited by Mitch, the counselors told him about clients. Only once did a counselor tell Mitch that the counselor preferred not to talk with him about drug court or the counselor's clients.

FIELD ROLES AND RELATIONS

Field researchers' social positions in their scenes and the relations they develop with the participants in their scenes affect what they observe and experience (Adler, 1985; Lofland & Lofland, 1995). Their roles and relations affect the understandings they develop. Being the program coordinator in two of the three drug courts that we studied, the courts that provided the great bulk of the observations, crucially affected what Mitch observed and experienced. Mitch was part of the phenomenon we were studying! He had significant emotional, professional and career interests in the success of these drug courts. His insider position provided opportunities and obstacles as a field researcher.

Mitch had great access to the other professional participants in drug court and to the places where they did their drug court work. As coordinator, he directly experienced being a professional in drug court. He was not only observing the behavior and conversations of other drug court professionals or talking with them about their experiences and reasoning, he was living it (Bochner & Ellis, 2002; Ellis, 2004).

Being a drug court coordinator also posed some obstacles for Mitch's fieldwork. First, his position put him in a place of authority over the drug court applicants and clients and over the treatment providers.

As explored earlier in the book, as drug court coordinator, Mitch met with potential clients and was crucially involved in deciding who to admit or reject. He discussed the clients' performance in the drug court treatment programs with the treatment staff. He informed the drug court judge of the clients' performance and recommended to the court what might be done concerning the promotion, punishment, removal and graduation of the clients. He exercised significant authority over the clients' participation in drug court.

Mitch also exercised some authority over the treatment providers. He contracted with the treatment providers for treatment services for the drug court clients and monitored the contracts.

Mitch's position of authority over clients and, to a lesser extent, over treatment providers meant that drug court applicants and clients and group counseling sessions between the treatment counselors and the clients were not easily available to him as they would not be to any coordinator with such authority. We knew that Mitch could not know the drug court applicants and clients beyond the limits of the official drug court relation that connects coordinators with drug-using offenders. A field researcher without a professional position in drug court may be more likely to come to know the drug-using offenders more intimately. Therefore, our work has not been a study of drug-using offenders but of drug court professionals who work with the offenders.

Mitch did not generally attend the group counseling in which drug court clients participated. At times when he did attend in his role of coordinator, the clients appeared agitated as if some problem had occurred. As program coordinator, Mitch typically attended only when a problem was occurring in group counseling!

Second, Mitch's personal and professional investment and experience in drug court and drug counseling may have led to several challenges in conducting this study. While our intent was never to criticize drug court, taking a questioning stance in which the working of drug court is not taken for granted but explored to understand how it is done can be more difficult when the lead researcher knows, likes and respects the professionals in drug court, values drug court, and wishes to appear capable. Mitch was concerned that he may offend his colleagues and undermine his commitment to drug court through what he learned and wrote (Fine, 1993). When field researchers try to explore and explain what people do in a scene, such explanations may be taken as critical by the participants if the researchers do not explicitly endorse the participants' actions and perspectives. Mitch employed several strategies to ensure analytic honesty. Over the years of the project, staff changed with new counselors and lawyers frequently replacing veterans. Close-working relationships were ruptured with transfers and departures. With over five years of observations a variety of staff appears and then disappears in fieldnotes. Since the observations were spread over many professionals, the likelihood of any one person feeling targeted or betrayed was lessened. The interviews with judges, coordinators and counselors provided each an opportunity to provide their story; another strategy. While Mitch did not share fieldnotes with each participant, he did share analysis and working concepts. Each staff could then correct Mitch's assertions if he was inaccurate. Finally, of all those staff discussed in this project, Mitch is most prominent. This was an early deliberate decision. If Mitch was going to offend a coworker he was also going to reveal his own foibles and acts.

As an experienced and heavily invested professional insider in drug court, Mitch had challenges in noticing the mundane in drug court and in reflecting on his observations and experiences. For example, Mitch needed to work hard just to hear colleagues or himself utter such mundane terms as "hit bottom." Having a colleague, Paul, on the project who was an experienced field researcher but not a drug court professional helped Mitch to see the drug court world with "fresher eyes" than otherwise would have been so.

Mitch met continuously with Paul during the research. Their discussions, often involving Paul questioning Mitch about his observations and reflections, enabled Mitch to move beyond his surface-level self-reflection. For the first year or so of the project, Mitch also met with other graduate student field researchers and Paul so that each student could discuss her or his project and receive comments from others.

Through the frequent questioning and probing by Paul, Mitch became more deeply reflective and consistently more reflective about drug court–about his experiences as a field researcher and as a program coordinator. Mitch came to ask himself how he knew what he was telling Paul about drug court. He began to make himself aware of and wonder about his and other professionals' statements and actions in drug court that he typically would have taken for granted as program coordinator.

For example, a treatment counselor for drug court broadly stated in a staff meeting that a particular client would never complete the program, and if the client did, the staff would see him when he was rearrested. The client was nothing but a "dealer." As the counselor commented on the client, Mitch, as a researcher, wondered why the counselor was telling him his view of this client and why the counselor used the term "dealer." Mitch appeared as the program coordinator to the counselor, but was observing and thinking about this interaction as a researcher.

At other times, Mitch would comment to others in drug court and immediately become the researcher, wondering about his reasoning. For example, Mitch might tell other drug court professionals that he wanted to give the "kid" (i.e., client) a second chance. Suddenly, he became a researcher and wondered why he had used the term "kid" and why he wanted to give this client, who had been performing poorly, another chance. Mitch was making the world of drug court, which in important ways he had taken for granted and which, undoubtedly, the vast majority of drug court professionals have taken for granted, available for his–and our–inspection.

What Mitch "knew" as drug court coordinator became examined and, at times, not confirmed by Mitch as field researcher. For example, as coordinator, Mitch often commented that most discharges from the drug court program were due to the clients' quitting, not from being removed by the staff and judge. As researcher, he was less certain. Mitch collected some data on discharges and concluded that he had been wrong in what he "knew" as program coordinator about discharges from drug court.

Mitch increasingly became a drug court coordinator with a field researchers' inquisitive sensitivity. Through field researching drug court and continually discussing his investigation with his colleague, both the court (as understood by the coordinator) and the coordinator changed.

Mitch became more thoughtful and questioning of statements made by others or by him about drug court. For example, during training on drug-court management that Mitch and other professionals from drug courts throughout the country attended, the speaker stressed the need for transgender- and homosexual-based counseling. She commented on the need for halfway houses, employment skills training, and obtaining the "buy in" of all "treatment entities." A judge at Mitch's table commented, "That is true; we have to change people from the inside out." Raising his hand, Mitch asked whether any evidence exists that shows these services do improve the outcome for drug court clients. No, the trainer replied, but she thought these were good services. Mitch thought to himself that the speaker was likely just repeating the well-used "party line." Mitch also thought about the use of "buy in" and what it may have been intended to convey or obscure. He quickly wrote the judge's comments and wondered how the judge evaluated change and what characteristics the judged looked for. The questions Mitch raised and the thoughts he had concerning these mundane statements became possible as he increasingly became a field research-reflective drug court coordinator.

ETHICS

We were concerned to protect the confidentiality of the professionals and participants in drug court about whom we learned and to eliminate any potential harm that our field research study may pose. We took a variety of precautions in order to protect the confidentiality of clients and professionals in the drug courts we observed. All names of clients and professionals used in this work are pseudonyms. Identifying information such as the race, sex and age of the clients have been altered or left out if they were not critical for the analysis. Outsiders to these drug courts could not identify the people within these pages. Insiders, however, may be able to identify certain key actors.

To help protect confidentiality, we stressed informed consent. Mitch took several steps to obtain informed consent. He informed all the major professionals involved with drug court–judges, the prosecuting attorney, and treatment staff–of what he was doing and obtained their permission. Public defenders and deputy prosecuting attorneys typically knew of Mitch's research. Private attorneys, being less routinely involved in drug court than public defenders, were less likely to be aware of the research. Mitch always obtained permission from those he interviewed, even when interviewing them more than once.

We sought to protect the safety of the drug court clients in two ways. Mitch arranged so that all drug users admitted to the drug court program in Urban County were informed that the court was under academic study. Second, Mitch decided never to interview drug court applicants or clients in his role of field researcher. Observations of the clients were made in public areas such as courtrooms, waiting areas and parking lots. Public domain information such as police rap sheets or case documents presented in court, not protected information, was used. Consequently, we decided that Mitch would not seek informed consent from the drug court applicants or clients. This met the standards of our university, which reviewed the proposal for the research, and of our profession.

We were aware that Mitch had the opportunity to try to have a decision made affecting a drug court applicant or client in order to serve his interests as a field researcher. For example, he may have wished for a drug court client to remain in the program as he was intending to use the client's history in the program for a case study. Of course, he never did that. Had he wanted to do that, however, he would have had to convince the treatment staff, attorneys, and judge to accept his view. Drug court is a team effort. This lessened the chance that Mitch could successfully act out of his interests as a field researcher should those interests differ from his professional concerns as a coordinator. However, since his field research interests were to understand the workings of drug court, we do not believe that those interests were at odds with his professional concerns as coordinator for dealing effectively and fairly with drug-using offenders.

OBSERVING AND MAKING NOTES

Mitch used a variety of approaches for observing and recording his observations (and reflections) in notes over the years of the project. He began by making notes about whatever he observed in his daily activities as program coordinator that occurred to him as potentially interesting. During the course of the project, he became more focused in his observations and note-making. As Mitch and Paul developed tentative ideas about drug court, as Mitch reviewed and classified his notes, and as he created over time increasingly complex flow charts that showed the set of decisions made about applicants and clients in drug court, Mitch and Paul realized that Mitch had not written sufficiently about various topics that had become of interest. For example, early in the project, we realized that we did not have sufficient detail about what the drug court professionals, the judge and the clients said in court. This led to Mitch's taping seven drug court sessions.

As the project proceeded, Mitch increasingly focused his observations on the drug court in Urban County in which he was an administrator. Suburban County's drug court became a site to verify what he observed in Urban County's drug court rather than to be a separate study. Not originally intending to explore the drug court in Farming County, Mitch increased his attention to drug court in Farming County as he became interested in how a drug court may operate within a small community. As we began writing this book, Mitch continued to make field research observations and notes about Farming County's drug court into which the Urban County's drug court has been folded until he left his position as program coordinator for an academic position.

Mitch jotted key words and phrases as he observed or as he participated in drug court activities in order to help him type fuller notes as soon as possible after the event. If away from his office, he might make more extensive jottings when he returned to his car or tape-record fuller notes as he returned to his office. He kept a steno pad on his desk and filled several of them with notes of phone calls or hallway conversations with lawyers and other drug court participants.[4] During the study, Mitch produced more than 400 pages of single-spaced typed fieldnotes.

Seventeen drug court staff professionals across the three courts were significant participants in our investigation. The four drug court judges were white males, each with more than fifteen years of judicial experience. The lead author, the only program coordinator for the drug courts in Urban and Farming Counties, is a white male with more than twenty years of experience in drug counseling and now drug courts. Two program coordinators served Suburban County's drug court during our study–a white male lawyer who began the program and more recently a white female with several years of experience in drug treatment. Of the four public defenders involved in our study, two were black females and two were white females. Among the seven drug counselors who treated clients in the three programs, four were white females, two were black men, and one was a white male. Their experience as counselors ranged from a few years to more than twenty years. One white female and the white male were recovering addicts.[5]

Mitch taped six major interviews and conducted other interviews that he did not tape but about which he later created notes. Mitch interviewed all the counseling staff except one, two drug court judges, two program coordinators, two pubic defenders and one prosecutor. Often he heard that a specific counselor was leaving the treatment pro-

4. For three months, Mitch kept a log of his daily activities in thirty-minute increments in order to learn how his activities proceeded during the course of the day. While this particular set of notes never entered the analysis, it was an important step in moving from participant to observer and identified the variety of tasks involved in being a coordinator.

5. We have no evidence that the social characteristics of the counselors made a difference on how they handled clients. A recovering counselor was similar to a nonrecovering, as a female was to a male.

gram and arranged to interview that counselor. Mitch also repeatedly discussed drug court with three key informants, two treatment counselors and a program coordinator.

With the permission of the judge, Mitch audiotaped seven complete drug court sessions in Urban County and transcribed them. Mitch plugged into the courtroom's taping system, which is used for transcriptions. While Mitch was busy as the coordinator during court sessions, he occasionally jotted key words uttered by the judge, defendant or himself on court forms before him. With the permission of the drug-using applicants, Mitch also taped six intake sessions and transcribed them.

Mitch became increasingly attentive to recording the language used by drug court professionals, especially the terms and phrases used by staff in referring to failures and successes in drug court (Emerson, 1969; Spradley, 1979). The terms used by staff to characterize drug court clients pointed to the identities the staff attributed to the clients and about what they expected of clients.

Drug courts, like all organizations, use a wide variety of forms in the conduct of their business. As coordinator, Mitch created or had access to arrest warrants, application forms used by the coordinator when a drug-using offender applies to the program, official court records prepared by the coordinator for the judge, court notes prepared by treatment providers to inform the program coordinator of services provided to clients and the clients' participation in treatment, and more.

ANALYSIS

Field researchers create their understandings through analyzing their fieldnotes. Through reviewing and coding fieldnotes, writing memos about the codes and about our developing insights about drug court, and discussing all of this as it progressed, we created our understandings presented in the previous pages. Through coding, field researchers decide how to interpret a passage of fieldnotes as an instance of a category of phenomenon. The following excerpt from an early set of fieldnotes includes the term "sign" which became a code:

> Dan C. had been in jail for over three months. He told me he had been "clean" for some time and was active in NA (narcotics anonymous). During the interview he used several NA phrases that told me

he had been in NA. I thought it was a good sign.

Through memos, field researchers put on paper their thoughts and questions about a coded phenomenon, about its links to other phenomenon, and about any other ideas or hunches they develop. Coding and writing memos provide guidance for further observations. Codes and hunches created earlier in the project may be kept, extended, modified, or rejected. From training, imagination and discussion, field researchers develop codes to help them make sense of their fieldnotes and of their scene (Emerson, Fretz, & Shaw, 1995; Glaser & Strauss, 1967; Lofland & Lofland, 1995).

Mitch initially coded his fieldnotes in order to place them within a flow chart that depicted how drug court professionals process drug-using offenders from the beginning to the end of drug court. He created seventy-two codes. Twenty-three of those codes, for example, were used to depict the complexity of the admission process. Later, Mitch created codes to represent more generic processes through which drug court participants interacted.

Coding of the notes was assisted through the use of a computer program, QSR N5 (Richards, 2000). The researcher creates the codes. The computer program helps the researcher attach codes to passages in the researcher's field notes and then retrieve and sort the passages quickly and efficiently. Mitch found the computer program to be immensely helpful in working with the hundreds of pages of fieldnotes that he wrote.

CONCLUSION

Through collaborative field research approach for more than five years, we explored three drug courts in a southeastern state. Even as we began to write this book, Mitch continued to make observations and write fieldnotes in his position as program coordinator in the combined Urban County and Farming County drug court. Being the program coordinator, provided Mitch an insider's opportunity for observing and experiencing drug court. Being the coordinator also posed challenges in exploring drug court. Some of these challenges, such as the potential for taking for granted what was occurring, were addressed through extensive and continuing discussions with his collaborator, Paul, an experienced field researcher who was an outsider to drug court. Team field research can often be fruitful (Douglas, 1977).

We have briefly described how we conducted this collaborative field research exploration of drug court. While brief, our discussion may provide the reader confidence in what we wrote about drug court. The greatest confidence in what we wrote will come from readers judging whether what we wrote makes sense of their experiences in drug court, of what they know about drug court, or what they know about other organizations in which the staff members create moral identities for the clients they serve. The value in our work will come from how the readers use it.

REFERENCES

Adler, P. A. (1985). *Wheeling and dealing: An ethnography of an upper-level drug dealing and smuggling community*. Columbia University Press: New York.

Alabama, University of (2001). *Breaking the cycle*. Birmingham: Graduate School University of Alabama, Birmingham.

Alexandrova, A. (2004). *AIDS, drugs and society*. New York: International Debate Education Association.

Anonymous, A. (2001). *Alcoholics anonymous: The big book* (Vol. 4th Edition). New York: Alcoholics Anonymous World Services, Inc.

Banks, D., & Gottfredson, D. C. (2004). Participation in Drug Treatment Court and Time to Rearrest. *Justice Quarterly, 21*(3), 637–658.

Bedrick, B., & Skolnick, J. (1999). From "Treatment" to "Justice" in Oakland, California. In W. C. Terry (Ed.), *The early drug courts: Case studies in judicial innovation* (pp. xi, 191). Thousand Oaks, CA: Sage Publications.

Belenko, S. (2001). *Research on drug courts: A critical review, 2001 update*. New York: National Center on Addiction and Substance Abuse at Columbia University.

Belenko, S., Peugh, J., & Menedez, D. (2002). *Trends in substance abuse and treatment needs among inmates*, Final Report (Report). New York: The National Center on Addiction and Substance Abuse.

Belenko, S. R. (2000). *Drugs and drug policy in America: A documentary history*. Westport, CT: Greenwood Press.

Bell, N. M., & Campbell, M. L. (2003). A child's death: Lessons from health care providers texts. *Journal of Sociology and Social Welfare, 30*(1), 113–126.

Bentley, P. (2005, Fall 2005). An international take on drug treatment courts. *NADCP News, 12*, 28.

Berman, G., & Feinblatt, J. (2001). Problem-solving courts: A brief primer. *Law and Policy, 23*(2).

Berman, G., & Feinblatt, J. (2005). *Good courts: The case for problem-solving justice*. New York: The New Press.

Black, D. J. (1989). *Sociological justice*. New York: Oxford University Press.

Bochner, A. P., & Ellis, C. (2002). *Ethnographically speaking: Autoethnography, literature and aesthetics*. Walnut Creek, CA: Altamira.

Boldt, R. (2002). The Adversary system and the attorney role in the drug court. In J. Nolan (Ed.), *Drug courts in theory and in practice*. New York: Aldine de Gruyter.

Boren, J. J., Onken, L. S., & Carroll, K. M. (Eds.). (2000). *Approaches to drug abuse counseling*. Washington, D.C.: National Institute on Drug Abuse, Division of Treatment and Research Development, Behavioral Treatment Development Branch.

Borg, M. (2000). Drug testing in organizations: Applying Horwitz's theory of effectiveness of social control. *Deviant Behavior, 21*(2), 123-154.

Bouffard, J., & Taxman, F. (2004). Looking Inside the "Black Box" of Drug Court Treatment Services Using Direct Observations. *Journal of Drug Issues, 34*(1), 195–218.

Braithwaite, J. (1989). *Crime, shame, and reintegration.* Cambridge Cambridgeshire; New York: Cambridge University Press.

Brewster, M. P. (2001). An evaluation of the Chester County (PA) Drug Court Program. *Journal of Drug Issues, 31*(1), 177–206.

Bureau of Justice Assistance, Drug Court Clearing house Project (2004). *Recidivism and other findings reported from selected evaluations of adult drug court programs published: 2000 - present.* Washington, D.C.: School of Public Affairs: American Univeristy.

Burns, S. L., & Peyrot, M. (2003). Tough love: Nurturing and coercing responsibility and recovery in California drug courts. *Social Problems, 50*(3), 416–438.

Cary, P. L. (2004). *Urine Drug Concentrations: The Scientific Rationale for Eliminating the Use of Drug Test Levels in Drug Court Proceedings.* Alexandria, VA: National Drug Court Institute.

Cooper, C. (2001). *Drug Court Activities Update: Summary Information on all Programs and Detailed Information on Adult Drug Courts* [Internet]. Office of Justice Programs; Drug Court Clearinghouse and Technical Assistance Project. Retrieved February 26, 2003, from the World Wide Web: http://www.american.edu/justice/publications/allcourtactivity.pdf

Cooper, C. (2003). Summary of Drug Court Activity by State and County [Internet]. American University, Drug Court Clearinghouse. Retrieved November 17, 2003, 2002, from the World Wide Web: http://spa.ward.american.edu/justice/publications/adultchart.pdf

Cooper, C. (2005). *Drug Court Activity Update: January 1, 2005* [Internet]. American Uni-versity, Drug Court Clearinghouse. Retrieved June 23, 2006, from the World Wide Web: http://spa.ward.american.edu/justice/publications

DeJong, C., & Wish, E. D. (2000). Is it Advisable to Urine test Arrestees to Assess Rick of Rearrest? A comparison of Self-Report and Urinalysis-Based measures of Drug Use. *Journal of Drug Issues, 30*(1), 133–146.

Deschenes, E., & Greenwood, P. (1994). Maricopa County's Drug Court: An innovative program for the first time drug offenders on probation. *Justice Systems Journal, 17*(1), 99–115.

Ditton, P. (1999). *Mental health and treatment of inmates and probationers* (special report). Washington, D.C.: Bureau of Justice Statistics.

Douglas, J. D. (1970). *Deviance & respectability; The social construction of moral meanings.* New York: Basic Books.

Douglas, J. D. (1977). Shame and deceit in creative deviance. In E. Sagarin (Ed.), *Deviance and Social Change* (p. 317). Beverly Hills, CA: Sage Publications.

Duneier, M. (1999). *Sidewalk* (1st ed.). New York: Farrar, Straus and Giroux.

Durose, M. R., & Langan, P. A. (2003). *Felony sentences in state courts, 2002.* Washington, D.C.: Office of Justice Programs.

Ellis, C. (2004). *The ethnographic: A methodological novel about autoethnography* (Vol. 13). Walnut Creek, CA: AltaMira Press.

Emerson, R. M. (1969). *Judging delinquents; context and process in juvenile court.* Chicago: Aldine Pub. Co.

Emerson, R. M., Fretz, R., & Shaw, L. (1995). *Writing ethnographic fieldnotes.* Chicago: University of Chicago Press.

Emerson, R. M., & Paley, B. (1992). Organizational horizons and complaint filing. In K. Hawkins (Ed.), *The Uses of Discretion* (pp. xiii, 431). Oxford, New York: Clarendon Press; Oxford University Press.

Farole, D., & Cissner, A. (2005). *Seeing eye to eye* (Research report). New York: Center for Court Innovation.

Fine, G. A. (1993). Ten lies of ethnography: Moral dilemmas of field research. *Journal of*

Contemporary Ethnography, 22(3), 267–294.
Flemming, R. B., Nardulli, P. F., & Eisenstein, J. (1992). *The craft of justice: Politics and work in criminal court communities.* Philadelphia: University of Pennsylvania Press.
Freeman-Wilson, K. (1999). *DWI Courts and DWI/Drug Courts: Reducing recidivism, Saving Lives* [Internet]. National Drug Court Institute. Retrieved June, 29, 2006, from the World Wide Web: www.ndci.org/dui.pdf
Freeman-Wilson, K., Tuttle, R., & Weinstein, S. P. (2001). *Ethical considerations for judges and attorneys in drug court.* Washington, D.C.: National Association of Drug Court Professionals.
Frohmann, L. (1991). Discrediting victims allegations of sexual assault: Prosecutorial account of case rejections. *Social Problems, 38*(2), 213–225.
Furst, T. R., Johnson, B. D., Dunlap, E., & Curtis, R. (1999). the stigmatized image of the "crack head": A sociocultural exploration of a barrier to cocaine smoking among a cohort of youth in New York City. *Deviant Behavior, 20*(2), 153–181.
Gallant, M. (1992). Slave runaways in Colonial Virginia: Accounts and status passage as collective process. *Symbolic Interaction, 15*(4), 389–412.
Garfinkel, H. (1956). Conditions of Successful Degradation Ceremonies. *American Journal of Sociology, 61*(5), 420–424.
Gately, I. (2001). *Tobacco: The story of how tobacco seduced the world* (1st American ed.). New York: Grove Press.
Glaser, B. G., & Strauss, A. L. (1965). Temporal aspects of dying as a non-scheduled status passage. *American Journal of Sociology, 71*, 48–59.
Glaser, B. G., & Strauss, A. L. (1967). *The discovery of grounded theory; strategies for qualitative research.* Chicago: Aldine Pub. Co.
Goffman, E. (1959). *The presentation of self in everyday life.* Garden City, New York: Doubleday Anchor Books.
Goldkamp, J. (1999). Challenges for research and innovation: When is a drug court not a drug court? In W. C. Terry (Ed.), *The early drug courts: Case studies in judicial innovation* (pp. xi, 191). Thousand Oaks, CA: Sage Publications.
Goldkamp, J. S. (1999). The Origin of the Treatment Drug Court in Miami. In W. C. Terry (Ed.), *The early drug courts: Case studies in judicial innovation* (pp. xi, 191). Thousand Oaks, CA: Sage Publications.
Goldkamp, J. S., & Weiland, D. (1993). *Assessing the Impact of Dade's County's Felony Drug Court.* Washington, DC: National Institute of Justice.
Goldkamp, J. S., White, M. D., & Robinson, J. B. (2001). Do drug courts work? Getting inside the drug court black box. *Journal-of-Drug-Issues, 31*(1), 27–72.
Goode, D. (1984). Socially produced identities, intimacy and the problem of competence among the retarded. In L. Barton & S. Tomlinson (Eds.), *Special education and social interests* (pp. ii–259). New York: Croom Helm; Nichols Pub. Co.
Gottfredson, D. C., & Exum, M. L. (2002). The Baltimore City Drug Treatment Court: One-Year Results from a Randomized Study. Journal of Research in Crime and Delinquency, 39(3), 337-356.
Gottfredson, D. C., Kearley, B. W., Najaka, S. S., & Rocha, C. M. (2005). The Baltimore City drug court: Three-year self-reported outcome study. *Evaluation Review, 29*(1), 42–64.
Gubrium, J. F., & Holstein, J. A. (2001). *Institutional selves: Troubled identities in a postmodern world.* New York: Oxford University Press.
Haigney, L. (1990, June 19, 1990). First time drug offenders get second chance at clean slate. *Miami Herald*, pp. 1–B.
Harris, C. (1980). When marriage ends: A study in status passage. *British Journal of Sociology, 31*(1), 129–131.
Harris, L. D. (1995). The validity on self-reported drug use. *Journal of Drug Issues, 25*(1), 91–111.

Hawkins, K. (1992). *The uses of discretion.* Oxford, New York: Clarendon Press; Oxford University Press.

Hawks, R. L., & Chiang, C. N. (1986). *Urine testing for drugs of abuse* (NIDA Research Monograph 73). Washington, D.C.: National Institute of Drug Abuse.

Higgins, P. (1994). *Sociological wonderment: The puzzles of social life.* Los Angeles: Roxbury.

Higgins, P. (1998). *Thinking about deviance.* Dix Hills: General Hill.

Higgins, P. C. (1985). *The rehabilitation detectives: Doing human service work.* Beverly Hills, CA: Sage Publications.

Hiller, M., Knight, K., Leukefeld, C., & Simpson, D. (2002). Motivation as a predictor of therapeutic engagement in mandated residential substance abuse treatment. *Criminal Justice and Behavior, 29*(1), 56–75.

Hines, L. (2003, January 4, 2003). Drug courts help addicts gain control over their lives. *The State*, pp. A–1.

Hirschi, T. (1969). *Causes of delinquency.* Berkeley: University of California Press.

Hoffman, M. (2002a). The Denver drug court and its unintended consequences. In J. Nolan (Ed.), *Drug courts in theory and in practice* (pp. xvi, 264). New York: Aldine de Gruyter.

Hoffman, M. (2002b). Therapeutic jurisprudence, Neo-rehabilitationism, and judicial collectivism: The least dangerous branch becomes most dangerous. *Fordham Urban Law Journal, 29*(5), 2063–2098.

Holstein, J. A. (1993). *Court-ordered insanity: Interpretive practice and involuntary commitment.* New York: Aldine de Gruyter.

Hora, P., Schma, W., & Rosenthal, J. (1999). Therapeutic jurisprudence and the drug court moment: Revolutionizing the criminal justice system's response to drug abuse and crime in America. *Notre Dame Law Review, 74*(2), 439–537.

Hubner, F. (1983). Transition into occupation life: Environment and sex differences regarding status passage from school to work. *Adolescence, 18*(71), 709–723.

Huddleston, C. W., Wilson-Freeman, K., Marlowe, D. B., & Roussell, A. (2005). *Painting the picture: A national report card on drug courts and other problem solving court programs in the United States.* Alexandra, VA: National Drug Court Institute.

Inciardi, J. A. (1992). *The war on drugs II: The continuing epic of heroin, cocaine, crack, crime, AIDS, and public policy.* Mountain View, CA: Mayfield Pub. Co.

Inciardi, J. A., McBride, D. C., & Rivers, J. E. (1996). *Drug control and the courts.* Thousand Oaks, CA: Sage Publications.

Institute, National Drug Court (2004). Drug courts today. National Drug Court Association. Retrieved May 4, 2004, from the World Wide Web: http://www.ndci.org/courtfacts.htm

Jellinek, E. M. (1960). *Disease concept of alcoholism.* New Haven: Hillhouse Press.

Joe, G. W., Simpson, D. D., & Broome, K. M. (1998). Effects of readiness for drug abuse treatment on client retention and assessment process. *Addiction, 93*(8), 1177–1190.

Joe, G. W., Simpson, D. D., & Broome, K. M. (1999). Retention and patient engagement models for different treatment modalities in DATOS. *Drug and Alcohol Dependence, 57*(2), 113–125.

Johnson, K. (1998, May 15, 1998). A 5-time washout, this addict broke the cycle. *USA Today*, p. 12A.

Jorgensen, D. L. (1989). *Participant observation: A methodology for human studies.* Newbury Park, CA: Sage Publications.

Kadden, R., Carroll, K., Donovan, D., Cooney, N., Monti, P., Abrams, D., Litt, M., & Hester, R. K. (Eds.). (1995). *Cognitive-behavioral coping skills therapy manual* (Vol. 3). Rockville: National Institute on Alcohol Abuse and Alcoholism.

Kellehear, A. (1990). The near-death experience as status passage. *Social Science and Medicine, 31*(8), 933–939.

Knudsen, H. K., Roman, P. M., & Johnson, J. A. (2004). The management of workplace deviance: Organizational responses to employee drug use. *Journal of Drug Issues, 4*(1), 121–144.

Liebow, E. (1993). *Tell them who I am: The lives of homeless women.* New York: Freepress.

Link, B., & Milcarek, B. (1980). Selection factors in the dispensation of therapy: The matthew effect in the allocation of mental health resources. *Journal of Health and Social Behavior, 21*(3), 279–290.

Lobdell, J. (2004). *This strange illness: Alcoholism and Bill W.* New York: Aldine de Gruyter.

Lofland, J., & Lofland, L. H. (1995). *Analyzing social settings: A guide to qualitative observation and analysis* (3rd ed.). Belmont, CA: Wadsworth.

Longshore, D., Turner, S., Wenzel, S., Morral, A., Harrell, A., Mcbride, D., Deschenes, E., & Iguchi, M. (2001). Drug courts: A cconceptual framework. *Journal of Drug Issues, 31*(1), 7–26.

Loseke, D. (1995). Appealing appeals: Constructing moral worthiness, 1912–1917. *The Sociological Quarterly, 36*(1), 61–77.

Mackinem, M. (2003a). *Completers vs. Non-completers.* Unpublished manuscript, Columbia.

Mackinem, M. (2003b). *Judging clients: The creation of moral identity in a drug court.* Unpublished Ph.D. Dissertation, University of South Carolina, Columbia, South Carolina.

Mackinem, M., & Higgins, P. (2007). Tell me about the test: The construction of truth and lies in drug court. *Journal of Contemporary Ethnography, 36*(3), 223–251.

Marlowe, D. B., Festinger, D. S., & Lee, P. A. (2004). The Judge is a key component of drug court. *Drug Court Review, 4*(2), 128.

Marlowe, D. B., Festinger, D. S., Lee, P. A., & Dugosh, K. L. (2006). Matching judicial supervision to clients risk status in drug court. *Crime & Delinquency, 52*(1), 52–76.

Mather, L. M. (1979). *Plea bargaining or trial? The process of criminal-case disposition.* Lexington, MA: Lexington Books.

McConville, M., & Mirsky, C. (1995). Guilty pleas courts: A social disciplinary model of criminal justice. *Social Problems, 42*(2), 216–234.

McCoy, C. (1993). *Politics and plea bargaining: Victims' rights in California.* Philadelphia: University of Pennsylvania Press.

McIntosh, J., & McKeganey, N. (2000). Addict's narratives of recovery from drug use: constructing a non-addict identity. *Social Science and Medicine, 50,* 1501–1510.

Melnick, G., Deleon, G., Hawke, J., & Jainchill, N. (1997). Motivation and readiness for therapeutic community treatment among adolescents and adult substances abusers. *American Journal of Drug and Alcohol Abuse, 23*(4), 485–506.

Mikkelson, B., & Mikkelson, D. P. (2003, May 14, 2003). *Urban legends reference page* [Internet]. Mikkleson, Barbara and David P. Retrieved May 23, 2005, from the World Wide Web: http://www.snopes.com/horrors/drugs/linklttr.htm

Miller, G., & Holstein, J. A. (1996). *Dispute domains and welfare claims: Conflict and law in public bureaucracies.* Greenwich, CT: Jai Press.

Miller, J. M., & Shutt, J. E. (2001). Considering the need for empirically grounded drug court screening mechanisms. *Journal of Drug Issues, 31*(1), 91–106.

Morgan, H. W. (1981). *Drugs in America: A social history, 1800–1980* (1st ed.). Syracuse: Syracuse University Press.

Murray, T. (1999). Personal conversation. In M. Mackinem (Ed.). Columbia.

Musto, D. F. (1999). *The American disease: Origins of narcotic control* (3rd ed.). New York: Oxford University Press.

Musto, D. F., & Korsmeyer, P. (2002). *The quest for drug control: Politics and federal policy in a period of increasing substance abuse, 1963–1981.* New Haven: Yale University Press.

NADCP, National Association of Drug Court Professionals. (1999). National Drug Court Week: Field Kit. Alexandria, Virginia.

National Institute of Justice (2006). Drug courts: The second decade. In U. D. O. Justice (Ed.) (p. 38): National Institute of Justice/NCJRS.

National Drug Court Institute (2004). Drug Courts Today. National Drug Court Association. Retrieved May 4, 2004, from the World Wide Web: http://www.ndci.org/courtfacts.htm

NIDA. (2000). *Approaches to drug abuse counseling.* Washington, D.C.: National Institute of Health.

Nolan, J. (2003). Redefining criminal courts: Problem solving and the meaning of justice. *American Criminal Law Review, 40*(4), 1541–1565.

Nolan, J. L. (1998). *The therapeutic state: Justifying government at century's end.* New York: New York University.

Nolan, J. L. (2001). *Reinventing justice: The American drug court movement.* Princeton, NJ: Princeton University Press.

Nolan, J. L. (2002). *Drug courts in theory and in practice.* New York: Aldine de Gruyter.

Office, Drug Court Program. (1997). Defining Drug Courts: The Key Components. In O. o. J. Programs (Ed.). Washington, D.C.: Government Printing Office.

Office, Government Accountability (1997). *Drug courts: Overview of growth, characteristics, and results GAO/GGD-97-106.* Retrieved September 13, 2002, from the World Wide Web: http://www.gao.gov/archive/1997/gg97106.pdf

Peele, S. (1989). *Diseasing of America: Addiction treatment out of control.* Lexington, MA: Lexington Books.

Peters, R. H., Haas, A. L., & Murrin, M. R. (1999). Predictors of Retention and Arrest in Drug Courts. *National Drug Court Institute Review, 2*(1), 33–60.

Peters, R. H., Hass, A. L., & Hunt, W. M. (2001). Treatment "dosage" effects in drug court programs. *Journal of Offender Rehabilitation, 33*(4), 63–72.

Peters, R. H., Hass, A. L., & Murrin, M. R. (1999). Predictors of retention and arrest in drug courts. *National Drug Court Institute Review, 2*(1), 30–58.

Peters, R. H., & Murrin, M. R. (2000). Effectiveness of treatment-based drug courts in reducing criminal recidivism. *Criminal Justice and Behavior, 27*(1), 72–96.

Peyrot, M. (1985). Coerced voluntarism: The micropolitics of drug treatment. *Urban Life, 13*(4), 343–365.

Project, Drug Court Clearinghouse. Bureau of Justice Assistance (2004). *Recidivism and other findings reported from selected evaluations of adult drug court programs published: 2000 - present.* Washington, D.C.: School of Public Affairs: American University.

Prottas, J. M. (1979). *People processing: The street-level bureaucrat in public service bureaucracies.* Lexington, MA: Lexington Books.

Quinn, M. C. (2000). Whose team am I on anyway? Musings of a public defender about drug treatment court practice. *N. Y. U. Review of Law and Social Change, 26*(37), 37–75.

Reinarman, C., & Levine, H. G. (1997). The crack attack: Politics and media in the crack scare. In C. Reinarman & H. G. Levine (Eds.), *Crack in America: Demon drugs and social justice* (pp. xvi, 388). Berkeley: University of California Press.

Rempel, M., Kralstein-Fox, D., Cissner, A., Cohen, R., Labriola, M., Farole, D., Bader, A., & Magnani, M. (2003). *The New York State Drug Court Evaluation.* New York: Center for Court Evaluation.

Richards, L. (2000). *Using N5 in Qualitative Research* (1 ed.). Bundoora, Australia: QSR International.

Ripton, K. (2000, March 10, 2000). A life changed: The anatomy of a drug court. *Chronicle-Independent,* p. 1.

Roth, J. (1972). Some contingencies of the moral evaluation and control of clientele: The case of the hospital emergency service. *American Journal of Sociology, 77*(5), 839–856.

Rottman, D., & Casey, P. (2000). Therapeutic jurisprudence and the emergence of problem-solving courts. *Alternatives to Incarceration*, 27–30.

Roy, W. G. (2001). *Making societies.* Thousand Oaks: Pine Forge Press.

Samenow, S. E. (1984). *Inside the criminal mind.* New York: Times Books.

Sanders, W. B. (1976). *Juvenile delinquency.* New York: Praeger.

Sandstorm, K. L., Martin, D. D., & Fine, G. A. (2003). *Symbols, selves, and social reality: A symbolic interactionist approach to social psychology and sociology.* Los Angeles: Roxbury.

Schiff, M., & Terry, W. C. (1997). Predicting graduation from Broward County's dedicated drug treatment. *Justice Systems Journal, 19*(3), 291–310.

Scott, M., & Lyman, S. (1970). Accounts, deviance and social order. In J. D. Douglas (Ed.), *Deviance & respectability: The social construction of moral meanings* (p. 468). New York: Basic Books.

Scott, R. A. (1967). The selection of clients by social welfare agencies, the case of the blind. *Social Problems, 14*(3), 248–457.

Senjo, S., & Leip, L. (2001). Testing and developing theory in drug court: A four-part logit model to predict program completion. *Criminal Justice Policy Review, 12*(1), 66–87.

Simpson, D., & Joe, G. W. (1993). Motivation as a predictor of early drop-out from drug abuse treatment. *Psychotherapy, 30*, 357–368.

Slobogin, C. (1995). Therapeutic jurisprudence: Five dilemmas to ponder. *Public Policy and the Law*, 193–196.

Snow, D. A., & Anderson, L. (1993). *Down on their luck: A study of homeless street people.* Berkeley: University of California Press.

Southern Methodist University (2002). *Evaluation of the divert court.* Dallas: Dallas County Divert Court.

Spinak, J. M. (2003). Why defenders feel defensive: The defender's role in problem solving courts. *American Criminal Law Review, 40*(4), 1617–1622.

Spohn, C., Piper, R. K., Martin, T., & Frenzel, E. D. (2001). Drug courts and recidivism: The results of an evaluation using two comparison groups and multiple indicators of recidivism. *Journal of Drug Issues, 31*(1), 149–176.

Spradley, J. P. (1979). *The ethnographic interview.* New York: Holt, Rinehart and Winston.

Stafford, M., & Warr, M. (1993). A reconceptualization of general and specific deterrence. *Journal of Research in Crime and Delinquency, 30*(2), 123–135.

Tauber, J., & Snavely, K. (1997). *Drug courts: A research agenda* (pamphlet). Alexandria, VA: National Drug Court Institute.

Tauber, J., Weinstein, S. P., Allen, C., & Lieupo, K. (2000). *Resource and funding guide.* Alexandria, VA: National Association of Drug Court Professionals.

Taxman, F. (1999). Unraveling "What Works" for Offenders in Substance Abuse Treatment Services. *National Drug Court Institute Review, 2*(2), 93–134.

Taylor, B. G., Fitzgerald, N., Hunt, D., Reardon, J. A., & Brownstein. (2001). *ADAM preliminary 2000 findings on drug use and drug markets.* In N. I. o. Justice (Ed.). Washington, D.C.

Terry, W. C. (1999a). *Broward County's dedicated drug treatment court: From postadjudication to diversion.* In W. C. Terry (Ed.), The early drug courts: case studies in judicial innovation (pp. xi, 191). Thousand Oaks: Sage Publications.

Terry, W. C. (1999b). *The early drug courts: Case studies in judicial innovation.* Thousand Oaks, CA: Sage Publications.

Tims, F. M., De Leon, G., Jainchill, N., & National Institute on Drug Abuse. (1994). *Therapeutic community: Advances in research and application.* Rockville, MD: U.S. Dept. of Health and Human Services Public Health Service National Institutes of Health National Institute on Drug Abuse.

Treatment, Center for Substance Abuse. (2005). *Substance Abuse Treatment for Persons With Co-occurring Disorders* (Treatment Improvement Protocol (TIP) Series, 42 (SMA) 05-3922).

Rockville, MD: Substance Abuse Mental Health Services Administration.

Ulmer, J. T., & Kramer, J. H. (1998). The use and transformation of formal decision-making criteria: Sentencing guidelines, organizational contexts, and case processing strategies. *Social Problems, 45*(2), 248–267.

University, S. M. (2002). *Evaluation of the divert court.* Dallas: Dallas County Divert Court.

Vogler, R. J. M. (1993). *The medicalization of eating: Social control in an eating disorders clinic.* Greenwich, CT: JAI Press.

Ward, D. A. (1980). Toward a normative explanation of "old fashion revivals." *Qualitative Sociology, 3*(1), 3–22.

Weiner, B. (1995). *Judgments of responsibility: A foundation for a theory of social conduct.* New York: Guilford Press.

Weppner, R. S. (1983). *The untherapeutic community: Organizational behavior in a failed addiction treatment program.* Lincoln: University of Nebraska Press.

Wexler, D. B. (1990). *Therapeutic jurisprudence: The law as a therapeutic agent.* Durham, N.C.: Carolina Academic Press.

White, W. L. (1979). *Themes in chemical prohibition.* Washington D.C.: National Insititute of Drug Abuse.

White, W. L. (1998). *Slaying the dragon: The history of addiction treatment and recovery in America.* Bloomington, IL: Chestnut Health Systems/Lighthouse Institute.

Yacoubian, G. S. (2000). Reassessing the need for urinalysis as a validation technique. *Journal of Drug Issues, 30*(2), 323–334.

Yochelson, S., & Samenow, S. E. (1976). *The criminal personality.* New York: J. Aronson.

Young, D., & Belenko, S. (2002). Program retention and perceived coercion in three models of mandatory drug treatment. *Journal of Drug Issues, 2*(1), 297–328.

INDEX